PENSACOLA

JOSHUA LAWRENCE KINSER

Contents

PENSACOLA

A culturally rich city, Pensacola has seen five flags—Spain, France, England, America, and the Confederacy—flown proudly at different historic moments in the past four centuries. The area is more widely known as a summer vacation destination—a picture-perfect beach retreat with deep turquoise waters and fine, white sand. It is also the site of numerous important forts as well as the Naval Air Station Pensacola, the launching point for the flight training of every American naval aviator, naval flight officer, and enlisted aircrew. It is home to the Blue Angels and the phenomenal, not-to-be-missed National Museum of Naval Aviation located on the Naval Air Station.

The city and the popular beach that sits on the barrier island of Santa Rosa are both much more casual than most areas along the Gulf Coast. It has plenty of upscale resorts and restaurants, but they seem to find a common thread with a laid-back, informal style that leaves pretentiousness behind and has managed to retain much of the Old Florida charm that has been lost in many of the cities and beaches to the south. Pensacola is infinitely more Southern in manner than most of the areas to the south—well, maybe with the exception of Everglades City. In Pensacola you will find the hospitality that you often associate with the South and food that is a unique blend of flavors inspired by a convergence of coastal American, Spanish, and Cajun cultures. You're just as likely to find menus offering deep-fried mullet with coleslaw, hush puppies, and a tall glass of sweet tea as you are grilled grouper with a mango sauce served with a side of black beans

HIGHLIGHTS

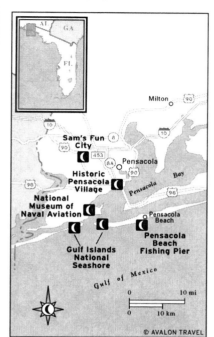

© AVALON TRAVEL

(Pensacola Beach Fishing Pier: The longest pier on the Gulf of Mexico is at the heart of festive, action-packed Pensacola Beach. You don't need a fishing license to wet a line (page 8).

(Gulf Islands National Seashore: The protected area has miles of delicate beach habitat along Santa Rosa Island, as well as Fort Pickens and other historic sights (page 9).

(Historic Pensacola Village: Stop off for sustenance at the Seville Quarter's Rosie O'Grady's before heading on to the cluster of 18th- and 19th-century museums and homes (page 13).

(National Museum of Naval Aviation: Find out why Pensacola is called the Cradle of Naval Aviation at this vast and spectacular museum (page 15).

(Sam's Fun City: At the center of Sam's Fun City is Surf City Water Park, where there are enough waterslides, wave pools, and water sprayers to keep the whole family cool even in the steamy Pensacola heat (page 17).

LOOK FOR **(** TO FIND RECOMMENDED SIGHTS, ACTIVITIES, DINING, AND LODGING.

and rice or a bowl of spicy New Orleans gumbo with a tray of raw oysters.

Pensacola has a long history. Native Americans left pottery shards and artifacts in the gentle coastal dunes here centuries before Tristán de Luna arrived with his fellow Spaniards in 1559. Tristán de Luna was the first to attempt a settlement in Pensacola, but violent hurricanes uprooted his attempts and sent the Spanish sailing south to St. Augustine, where they established North America's first European settlement. Even after this first exploratory settlement didn't take, Pensacola was settled by white Europeans very early on. It was

one of a handful of colonial period communities in the southeastern United States, its Seville Historic District one of the oldest and most intact in all of Florida. Within this small neighborhood is Old Christ Church, Florida's oldest church still standing in one place (1832), and St. Michael's Cemetery, deeded to Pensacola by the king of Spain in 1822. A walk through Historic Pensacola Village will give you insight into the area's history.

Pensacola has a strong military presence with Naval Air Station Pensacola and nearby Eglin Air Force Base; it is often called the Cradle of Naval Aviation. The free National Museum of

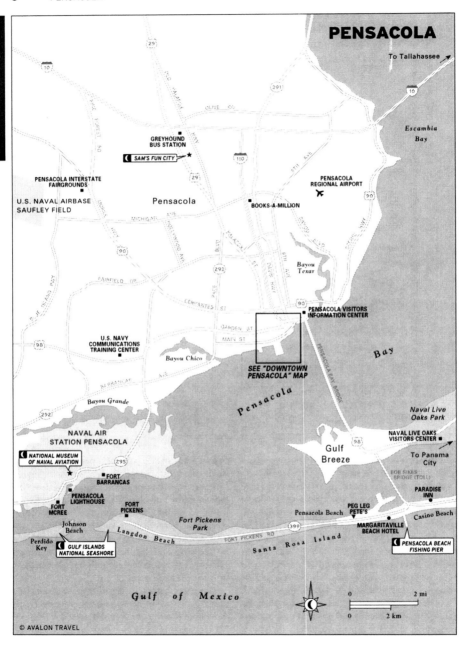

PENSACOLA

To Tallahassee

Escambia
Bay

GREYHOUND
BUS STATION

SAM'S FUN CITY

PENSACOLA
REGIONAL AIRPORT

PENSACOLA INTERSTATE
FAIRGROUNDS

Pensacola

U.S. NAVAL AIRBASE
SAUFLEY FIELD

BOOKS-A-MILLION

Bayou
Texar

FAIRFIELD DR

CERVANTES ST

PENSACOLA VISITORS
INFORMATION CENTER

U.S. NAVY
COMMUNICATIONS
TRAINING CENTER

GARDEN ST

MAIN ST

Bay

Bayou Chico

SEE "DOWNTOWN
PENSACOLA" MAP

Bayou Grande

Pensacola

Naval Live
Oaks Park

NAVAL AIR
STATION PENSACOLA

NAVAL LIVE OAKS
VISITORS CENTER

NATIONAL MUSEUM
OF NAVAL AVIATION

Gulf
Breeze

To Panama
City

BOB SIKES
BRIDGE (TOLL)

FORT
BARRANCAS

PENSACOLA
LIGHTHOUSE

PARADISE
INN

FORT
MCREE

FORT
PICKENS

Pensacola Beach

PEG LEG
PETE'S

Casino Beach

Johnson
Beach

Langdon Beach

Fort Pickens
Park

FORT PICKENS RD

MARGARITAVILLE
BEACH HOTEL

Perdido
Key

GULF ISLANDS
NATIONAL SEASHORE

Santa Rosa Island

PENSACOLA BEACH
FISHING PIER

Gulf   of   Mexico

0   2 mi

0   2 km

© AVALON TRAVEL

It made landfall as a Category III hurricane, wreaking particular havoc around Perdido Bay and Pensacola Beach. The area's bridges and roads sustained major damage, and locals say 99 percent of the buildings in the area were damaged, with a staggering 40 percent utterly destroyed or catastrophically damaged by the 130-mph winds and 10- to 12-foot storm surge.

Ivan the Terrible did its darnedest (causing an estimated $13 billion worth of damage, it's the fifth-costliest hurricane to ever strike the United States), but it's all back up to speed these days, although some road restoration in natural areas was complicated by the fact that they are habitat for endangered species—all work must be approved by the U.S. Fish and Wildlife Service and other government bodies.

PLANNING YOUR TIME

The best way to explore Pensacola is with a car, but you can get by with community transportation and taxis if you are planning on spending most of your time downtown and in the Pensacola Beach areas. If you want to use Pensacola as a home base and satellite out to the surrounding attractions, then you will want to rent a car. The Pensacola area is fairly spread out. The most popular area for accommodations is Pensacola Beach. Downtown Pensacola and the Perdido Key area come in a close second, with the downtown area being more historical in nature with several excellent bed and breakfasts and hotels, and the beaches having mostly chains and high-rise condos to choose from. As on most of the Panhandle, high season is April-August. The value season runs roughly August-March. Regardless of when you'd like to visit, make reservations in advance. Visitors at the naval base tend to fill the hotels nearest it. The greater Pensacola area can easily occupy you for three or four days with its historical attractions, beaches, and nature parks. If you want to really explore all the great beaches in the area, then plan for a week, two if you want to spend an extensive amount of time fishing, paddling, or generally sightseeing in Perdido, Gulf Shores, and Dauphin Island to the west

SCENIC DRIVE EAST ALONG GULF OF MEXICO

World's Whitest Beaches

The retro-style Pensacola Beach sign is a local landmark.

Naval Aviation, the third largest in the world, showcases the history of aviation through indoor and outdoor exhibits.

And then there are the beaches. Some are developed, fun, tourist beaches such as Pensacola Beach; others are more uninhabited. The Gulf Islands National Seashore cuts through this area, a 150-mile-long, discontinuous string of undeveloped barrier islands that begins at Santa Rosa Island and extends into Mississippi. Santa Rosa Island contains seven beautiful, undeveloped miles of beach, with clear water, white sandy beaches, lots of fish and wildlife, and fewer people crowding the pristine shores.

HURRICANES

Pensacola's location on the Panhandle makes it particularly vulnerable to hurricanes. Many storms over the years have made landfall here—a number during years before storms were named, and then Hurricane Juan in 1985, the devastating Hurricane Opal in 1995, and Hurricane Ivan on September 16, 2004.

or the forests, creeks, and rivers to the north. If you fly into Pensacola and rent a car, think about tacking on a couple of extra days to explore the Emerald Coast area just to the east.

For camping, head to the Gulf Islands National Seashore at Fort Pickens just west of Pensacola Beach, north to the Black Water and Coldwater Creek areas around Brewton, and west to Tarklin Bayou and Big Lagoon State Parks around Perdido. All of these areas offer excellent paddling, fishing, and hiking as well. The epicenter for fishing is in Pensacola Beach and the marinas surrounding the downtown areas, where most of the fishing charters run daily trips into offshore fishing spots. A favorite of serious anglers is a charter out to the *Oriskany,* an aircraft carrier that was sunk 24 miles offshore and is now utilized as an artificial reef and recreational dive spot.

I-10 is the main east-west interstate into the city with I-110 jutting out to the south and bringing visitors into the heart of downtown Pensacola. U.S. 98 primarily serves the beaches and connects the popular coastal areas of the region, while County Road 3999 or Via De Luna Drive serves as the main thoroughfare for Santa Rosa Island, the barrier island where Pensacola Beach, the Gulf Islands National Seashore, and Navarre Beach are located. The best beaches in the area include the stretch of Gulf Islands National Seashore between Pensacola Beach and Navarre, Casino Beach where you find the Pensacola Beach Gulf Fishing Pier, and the beaches at Big Lagoon State Park in Perdido.

Sports and Recreation

BEACHES

There are wonderful beaches here, all of which took a beating from Hurricane Ivan in 2004 and have now completely rebounded. The long stretch of the **Gulf Islands National Seashore** and the **Naval Air Station Pensacola** and **Eglin Air Force Base** farther east have imposed restrictions on commercial growth. The communities in the area set quotas on density and height restrictions on new construction. Thus, the more urban beachfront areas around Pensacola aren't littered with high-rise condos and resort hotels, and there's another six miles of utterly preserved seashore in the park. Still, the area had been recovering from Hurricane Opal for nine years when it got walloped, in nearly identical ways, by Hurricane Ivan in 2004.

Perdido Key is the westernmost island in the long chain of barrier islands that line the Panhandle's edge, an island that Florida shares with the state of Alabama. The developed beach areas are called **Orange Beach** and **Johnson Beach,** and the more natural part is **Perdido Key State Park** (15301 Perdido Key Dr., 15 miles southwest of Pensacola, off Hwy. 292, 850/492-1595, 8am-sundown daily, $3 honor system for beach, $4 for main park). These beaches provide some of the best swimming in the state—warm, clear water, gentle surf, long stretches of shallows. **Big Lagoon State Park** (12301 Gulf Beach Hwy., 15 miles southwest of Pensacola, off Hwy. 292, 850/492-1595, 8am-sundown daily, $6/vehicle, $20 camping, $10 boat launch fee) is located just across the bay from Perdido Key and offers tent, camp trailer, and RV sites. Take a short drive up the road and hike the nature trails at Tarkiln Bayou Preserve State Park.

Santa Rosa Island, just to the east, is one of the longest barrier islands in the world, stretching 50 miles from Pensacola Bay on its western side to Choctawhatchee Bay to its east. The beaches here are all fine, white quartz sand.

◖ Pensacola Beach Fishing Pier

Pensacola Beach (Pensacola Beach Visitor Information Center, 800/635-4803) itself covers much of the island, with restaurants, shops, and entertainment at their highest density near the Pensacola Beach Fishing Pier—at 1,471 feet long and 30 feet above the water, the pier is second behind the new Gulf Pier at Gulf

FAST TIMES

Addicted to speed? Pensacola has a couple of ways to scratch that itch. **Five Flags Speedway** (7451 Pine Forest Rd., on Hwy. 297 a mile south of Exit 2 on I-10, 850/944-8400, www.5flagsspeedway.com, dates and times vary, $10-20) was built in 1956, one of the oldest established short track racetracks still in existence. A high-banked asphalt oval, it is the fastest half-mile track in the country and home to the annual Snowball Derby (usually the first few days of December). The Snowball Derby is widely recognized as the country's premier short track Super Late Model event. The rest of the season features racing of different kinds, from the fire-breathing, fuel-injected, winged sprint cars of the United Sprint Car Series, to the Bombers, Spectators, Super Stocks, Vintage, and Pro Late Models. The track has attracted top drivers like Carl Yarborough and Rusty Wallace, and fans from all over.

Pensacola Greyhound Track (951 Dog Track Rd., off U.S. 98, 850/455-8595, www.pensacolagreyhoundpark.com, 7pm Fri.-Sat., 1pm Sun., free admission) offers the thrill of high-speed greyhound racing and the equally thrilling attendant betting. You can watch the races from an air-conditioned restaurant/lounge called the Kennel Club or from rail-side seats. The facility also has live and instant replay televisions throughout the complex.

State Park measuring 1,540 feet long. Crossing the two bridges from Pensacola to Santa Rosa Island, you'll be on Pensacola Boulevard—it splits left and right, but directly in front of you is Pensacola Beach. The area is rich with water-sport possibilities: parasailing, sailboarding, deep-sea fishing, Jet Skiing, and scuba diving. Pensacola Beach is open to the public, accessible by car or by ECAT bus or trolley. The fishing pier is open to the public 24 hours a day and costs $1 to walk on, $7.50 for adults to fish, children under six are free; you're likely to catch flounder, bonita, Spanish and king mackerel, and cobia. From its end you're likely to spot dolphins, sea turtles, and the occasional manatee.

At the corner of Pensacola Boulevard and Fort Pickens Road, which goes to the west, is **Casino Beach.** It is the heart of Pensacola Beach, named for an old beachside casino resort from 1933. The casino is long gone, but its beach ball water tank is still the beach's landmark. Casino Beach is home to the huge brick Gulfside Pavilion, site of numerous free concerts and events over the years. The beach has picnic tables, restrooms, restaurants, and souvenir shops. And just past the tollbooth onto the island, **Quietwater Beach,** on the Santa Rosa Sound side, is a gentle, shallow beach great for kids.

◖ Gulf Islands National Seashore

The **Gulf Islands National Seashore** (850/934-2622, $3/person or $8/vehicle for a 7-day pass) has numerous beaches along Santa Rosa Island. At its westernmost edge is **Fort Pickens Park,** maintained by the National Park Service. Fort Pickens Road was breached by Ivan in 2004 and then whomped the next year by Dennis, but has reopened to the public. The road is located in a sensitive habitat for nesting sea turtles and colonial shorebirds, so be sure not to park along the sandy road shoulder. This will also help you avoid getting your vehicle stuck and keep you from getting a park ranger-administered ticket.

Historic Fort Pickens is open for self-guided tours during daylight hours only. The fishing pier is open, and the Fort Pickens campground has 200 campsites equipped with water and electricity for $20 per night. Campers have access to running water, grills, picnic tables, and bathrooms with cold showers. Boaters planning to camp can unload their passengers and gear near Battery Langdon, located on the bay side of the island and west of the Ranger Station dock, and hike on the bike path or Fort Pickens Road to Loop A.

The J. Earle Bowden Way (Hwy. 399) on Santa Rosa Island connects Pensacola Beach

© JOSHUA LAWRENCE KINSER

Pensacola Beach Fishing Pier

with Navarre Beach. This road was also damaged by the two hurricanes but is now open again.

Within the Fort Pickens area is another beach called **Langdon Beach,** which has picnic tables, restrooms, and outdoor showers. The scenic bike path, going from Langdon Beach all the way to the fort, has been restored, as have the Dune Nature Trail and the Blackbird Marsh Nature Trail.

Also part of Gulf Islands National Seashore, **Opal Beach** is three miles east of Pensacola Beach. It is generally less populated than Pensacola Beach, offering restrooms, showers, and picnic pavilions, and is a great stop for hikers and bikers taking in the beautiful dune landscape between Pensacola Beach and Navarre Beach on the Seashore Trail or the South Santa Rosa Loop Trail. The Opal Beach area can also be reached by motorists via Highway 399, which runs parallel to the multiuse trail through the national seashore. From Pensacola Beach, drive east toward Navarre Beach on Highway 399. Opal Beach will be

on the Gulf side (right). From Navarre Beach, drive west toward Pensacola Beach on Highway 399. Opal Beach will on the Gulf side (left).

Navarre Beach

Navarre Beach is the easternmost beach on Santa Rosa Island. It's a family-friendly beach, with bathrooms, picnic facilities, and a fishing pier. The Navarre Beach County Park is 130 acres of beach, wetlands, and scrub, a third of which is set aside for nondevelopment in perpetuity. After lolling on the beach, the multiuse Seashore Bicycle Trail will carry you alongside dunes, forests, and the Gulf for a nice array of picturesque scenery.

FISHING AND DIVING

The area's had some losses, but also some gains. The Three Mile Bridge over Pensacola Bay has in recent years carried traffic alongside the long-abandoned U.S. 98 bridge. That bridge, prior to Hurricane Ivan, was used by local anglers as their huge personal fishing pier. Now much of that pier lies on the bottom of

Pensacola Bay. In 2010, the newly constructed fishing pier that runs alongside the Three Mile Bridge was completed, and anglers are back to reeling in their catches from Pensacola Bay. In general, fishing in the area has taken a huge upswing. The decommissioned aircraft carrier **USS Oriskany** was sunk as an artificial reef in the Gulf of Mexico 22.5 miles southeast of Pensacola Pass in May 2006. The navy committed $2.8 million for its preparation and deployment as a reef, the first time a ship of this size had been sunk for this purpose. The decommissioned Mighty O (32,000 tons and 911 feet), which saw action in Korea and Vietnam, sits in 212 feet of water. The *Oriskany* is the first navy ship cleaned following the EPA's 2004 policies ensuring artificial reefs are environmentally safe.

Anglers have already started to flock in large numbers to the greater Pensacola area. Even more enthusiastic than the anglers, though, are the divers. Divers can reach the top of the *Oriskany*'s superstructure or "island" at 60 feet, while its flight deck sits in 130 feet of water, below the depth of recreational divers but well within reach of specialty divers trained in deepwater diving. With year-round warm water temperatures (mid-80s in summer and mid-60s in winter) and visibility of 60-100 feet, it's tempting to divers.

Not surprising, then, that this has been used as the site of underwater weddings. Crystal and

Cooper Labenske were the first to literally take the plunge here, in May 2006. Pensacola Dive Company owner Captain Ron Beermünder officiated the underwater "I dos."

SPECTATOR SPORTS
Pensacola Wahoos

Pensacola has always had a love affair with their massive beach ball water tower on Pensacola Beach, now the town is embracing baseball with open arms at the **Pensacola Bayfront Stadium** (351 W. Cedar St.), the brand-new baseball and sports complex. It is primarily home to the **Pensacola Wahoos** (850/934-8444, www.milb.com, tickets $10-50), a Cincinnati Reds affiliate minor-league team, but the stadium occasionally hosts football games and concerts. Built right on Pensacola Bay just on the outskirts of downtown near the foot of the Three Mile Bridge, the new stadium quickly received accolades in the baseball community, including the Best Ballpark of 2012 award from baseballparks.com. The classic open-air stadium seats 5,038 fans and was designed by the same award-winning baseball stadium design firm that built the new Yankee Stadium, the Giant's AT&T Park, and completed the renovation of Wrigley Field for the Chicago Cubs. It's a beautiful ballpark in a stunning coastal setting and a great place to spend the evening after a fun day at Pensacola Beach just across the Three Mile Bridge.

Sights

Downtown Pensacola is awash in historical attractions, many of them clustered in one of several historic districts. For a fun way to explore the history of this area, take a two-hour guided tour on a Segway with **Emerald Coast Tours** (701 S. Palafox St., 850/417-9292, call to schedule tour, $65 adults, $60 students and military). Guide Nic Shuck gives you a crash course on operating one of the two-wheeled Segways before you embark on a high-speed excursion that explores the best historical sights and landmarks

in downtown Pensacola, including the Plaza De Luna where the Spanish officially handed over Florida to the United States. It's a great way to get yourself familiarized with the lay of the land when you first get into town—perfect for less mobile visitors who would rather not walk the long blocks of downtown—and along the way you'll learn the best spots for good eats and drinks. There are also night tours of the East Hill district (5:30pm and 7:30pm Sat. only, $45 adults, $40 students and military).

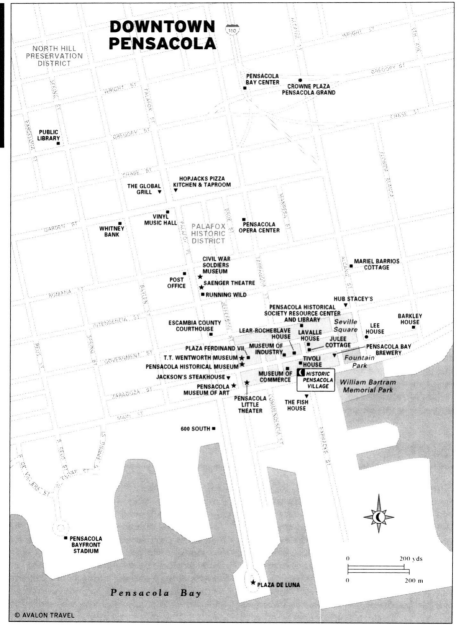

DOWNTOWN PENSACOLA

NORTH HILL
PRESERVATION
DISTRICT

PENSACOLA
BAY CENTER
CROWNE PLAZA
PENSACOLA GRAND

PUBLIC
LIBRARY

HOPJACKS PIZZA
KITCHEN & TAPROOM
THE GLOBAL
GRILL

VINYL
MUSIC HALL
WHITNEY
BANK
PALAFOX
HISTORIC
DISTRICT
PENSACOLA
OPERA CENTER

CIVIL WAR
SOLDIERS
MUSEUM
MARIEL BARRIOS
COTTAGE
POST
OFFICE
SAENGER THEATRE
RUNNING WILD

HUB STACEY'S

PENSACOLA HISTORICAL
SOCIETY RESOURCE CENTER
AND LIBRARY
Seville
Square
LEE
HOUSE
BARKLEY
HOUSE
ESCAMBIA COUNTY
COURTHOUSE
LEAR-ROCHEBLAVE
HOUSE
LAVALLE
HOUSE
JULEE
COTTAGE
PENSACOLA BAY
BREWERY
PLAZA FERDINAND VII
MUSEUM OF
INDUSTRY
T.T. WENTWORTH MUSEUM
Fountain
Park
TIVOLI
HOUSE
PENSACOLA HISTORICAL MUSEUM
MUSEUM OF
COMMERCE
HISTORIC
PENSACOLA
VILLAGE
JACKSON'S STEAKHOUSE
William Bartram
Memorial Park
PENSACOLA
MUSEUM OF ART
PENSACOLA
LITTLE
THEATER
THE FISH
HOUSE

600 SOUTH

PENSACOLA
BAYFRONT
STADIUM

0   200 yds

0   200 m

PLAZA DE LUNA

Pensacola Bay

SEVILLE SQUARE

The survivors of an early, thwarted attempt to settle Santa Rosa Island hightailed it to more solid ground and established a permanent settlement in 1752. After the French and Indian War of 1763, the British took west Florida and occupied the area, laying out a clean grid of houses. The Spanish, upon capturing Pensacola after that, kept the old town square intact but renamed the streets to reflect the new Spanish presence. So about 20 blocks of historic 18th- to 19th-century residential and business streets have Spanish names. It's a beautiful area with a mixture of Victorian, Spanish-, and French-influenced Gulf Coast-style cottages (these are often 1.5-story houses with steeply pitched gabled roofs and a deep front porch) centered on shady Seville Square Park.

The Seville Historic District makes for a wonderful afternoon of walking. First, I encourage a stop at **Seville Quarter** (130 E. Government St., 850/434-6211, 11am-3am, late night menus until 1am, $10-25, $3 Wed., $10 Thurs., $5 Fri. and Sat., free admission Sun.-Tues.) for live music, food, or a few cold drinks. Within this historic complex, down an east alleyway, stop into **Rosie O'Grady's** for some Dixieland jazz dueling pianos, a Flaming Hurricane, and the historic setting— it was built in 1871 as the Pensacola Cigar and Tobacco Company. Directly across from Rosie O'Grady's is the entrance to **Lili Marlene's World War I Aviators Pub,** once the Pensacola Printing Co., which for a long time was the oldest print shop in continuous operation in the country and the original home of the *Pensacola News Journal*. Beyond these, there are several other themed rooms in this entertainment and dining complex, outfitted with period antiques. The complex also has two inviting courtyards and a gift shop.

Historic Pensacola Village

Also part of the Seville Historic District, **Historic Pensacola Village** (850/595-5985, 10am-4pm Tues.-Sat., $6 adults, $5 seniors and active military, $3 children 4-16, children 3 and under free) is bounded by Government,

© JOSHUA LAWRENCE KINSER

Take a stroll through historic Seville Square in downtown Pensacola.

Taragona, Adams, and Alcanz Streets. The village consists of 20 properties in the Pensacola National Register Historic District. Ten of these properties are interpretive facilities open to the public: the Museum of Commerce, Museum of Industry, Julee Cottage, Lavalle House, Lear House, Dorr House, Old Christ Church, Weaver's Cottage, Tivoli House, and Colonial Archaeological Trail. Do them all if you've got the stamina—the guided house tour is the way to go. House tours are included in the admission price and leave from the Tivoli House at 11am, 1pm, and 2:30pm.

T. T. Wentworth Jr. Florida State Museum (Plaza Ferdinand, free admission) is an elaborate Renaissance Revival building that houses rotating exhibits on west Florida's history, architecture, and archaeology (kids will go more willingly if you tell them there's also a shrunken head on display). The **Museum of Commerce** (201 E. Zaragoza St.) is a brick turn-of-the-20th-century warehouse containing a reconstructed 1890s-era streetscape with a toy store; leather, hardware, music, and print shops; and horse-drawn buggies. The **Museum of Industry** (200 E. Zaragoza St.) houses an exhibit depicting several important 19th-century industries in west Florida: fishing, brickmaking, railroad, and lumber. It was the most recent to reopen, and features a variety of interactive displays teaching visitors about the area's natural resources and early industry.

The historic homes in the village include the **Lavalle House** (205 E. Church St.), an example of French Creole colonial architecture; the **Dorr House** (311 S. Adams St.), Greek Revival architecture furnished with fine antiques; and the **Lear-Rocheblave House** (214 E. Zaragoza St.), a two-story folk Victorian home with several furnished rooms. The **Barkley House** (410 S. Florida Blanca St.) is one of the oldest masonry houses in Florida, and the **Mariel Barrios Cottage** (204 S. Alcaniz St.) is owned and operated by the Pensacola Historic Preservation Society and exhibits household items and furnishings from Pensacola during the 1920s. The **Julee Cottage** (210 E. Zaragoza St.) is a museum classroom once owned by Julee Panton,

a free African American woman. The **Tivoli House** (205 E. Zaragoza St.) is a reconstructed version of an 1805 boarding- and gaming house and now houses the Historic Pensacola Village gift shop and ticket office.

After touring the homes, pick up the brochure for the **Colonial Archaeological Trail,** which was produced by the Archaeology Institute at the University of West Florida; it leads you through the ruins of the colonial commanding officer's house, the foundations of the officer-of-the-day's building, and the remains of what might have been a trader's home and warehouse just outside the western gate of the British fort built during the American Revolution.

Also, the **Pensacola Historical Museum** (115 E. Zaragoza St., 850/433-1559, 10am-4pm Tues.-Sat., free admission) is in the midst of the historic village, operated by the Pensacola Historical Society. It offers changing exhibits every year on topics of local history (currently that includes the Hotel San Carlos, Pensacola commemorative glass, sailors, snapper fishing, yellow fever, the West Florida Regional Library, and slaves at Fort Pickens). It also sponsors a deliciously eerie haunted house tour in October—see it if you can time your visit right.

PALAFOX HISTORIC DISTRICT

Palafox Historic District is another historic area downtown, contiguous with Seville Square, only just to the west of it. It runs up Palafox Street from Pensacola Bay in the south to about Wright Street in the north. Again, it's an area of beautiful homes and historic buildings with wide brick sidewalks. It's really the commercial heart of Pensacola, and it houses a couple of the area's big cultural draws.

The **Pensacola Museum of Art** (407 S. Jefferson St., 850/432-6247, 10am-5pm Tues.-Fri., noon-5pm Sat. and Sun., $5 adults, $2 students and active military, free admission on Tues.) is right at its center, with a wonderful space and intriguingly diverse visiting exhibits that range from the realistic sculptures of Duane Hanson to 20th-century Japanese printmaking. The permanent collection has minor works, most on paper, by some heavy hitters (largely 20th century) as well as lots of fine decorative glass. The museum is housed in what was the city jail (1906-1954), so there are sturdy bars on the windows.

Just around the corner you will find the **Vinyl Music Hall** (5 E. Garden St., 850/607-6758, www.vinylmusichall.com, tickets $7-50), the newest music and entertainment venue in town. What was once a historic Mason Lodge has been restored and remodeled into a hip music venue and bar. The intimate general admission venue is standing room only and is starting to draw large national acts mainly in the blues and rock genres like Dr. John and the Blues Travelers, but it mostly features national and regional alternative rock artists.

NORTH HILL PRESERVATION DISTRICT

Before you tire of all this history, another worthy walk is the North Hill Preservation District, which occupies 50 city blocks due north of the Palafox District, away from the water, bounded on the west by Reus and on the east by Palafox. On the National Register of Historic Places, the neighborhood is pretty much residential, with great examples of fully restored historic homes. You can't go inside unless you make friends, but some of the current owners are descendants of the original builders—Spanish nobility, lumber barons, French Creoles, and Civil War soldiers.

NAVAL AIR STATION PENSACOLA

Pensacola is known as the Cradle of Naval Aviation, a bold claim that can be authenticated through an exploration of one of the many sites open to the public at the Naval Air Station Pensacola and environs. To reach the historic mainland forts and the National Museum of Naval Aviation from the north, take Exit 7 off I-10 (Pine Forest Rd., Hwy. 297), go about 1.5 miles, and take a right onto Blue Angel Parkway. Then drive 12 miles to the west gate of the Naval Air Station. (Visitors without military stickers can *depart* only from the main entrance on Navy Blvd.)

◖ National Museum of Naval Aviation

If you're only going to devote time to one historic attraction in the greater Pensacola area, the **National Museum of Naval Aviation** (1750 Radford Blvd., NAS Pensacola, 850/453-2389, 9am-5pm daily, free admission, free parking, free tours) is it. It's one of the largest air and space museums in the world, with 160 restored aircrafts representing Navy, Marine Corps, and Coast Guard aviation. There's a seven-story, glass-and-steel atrium in which four A-4 Skyhawks are suspended in formation. You can stand on the flight deck of the USS *Cabot* and fly an F/A-18 mission in Desert Storm in a motion-based flight simulator. There's an IMAX theater ($8.75) with a film called *The Magic of Flight.* Before the government program was cut, the **Blue Angels** were based in Pensacola and had a practice area adjacent to the museum. You can't see their high-flying feats of aviation prowess any longer, but you can still get their autographs at the museum every Wednesday at 11:30am.

Pensacola Lighthouse

Also on the grounds of the Naval Air Station Pensacola, the **Pensacola Lighthouse** (Hwy. 292 S) follows on the heels of other lighthouses constructed in this area. The construction of the first Pensacola lighthouse, the Aurora Borealis, was completed in 1824, the first lighthouse on the Gulf Coast and the second lighthouse in Florida. It stood at the northern entrance of the bay near the present-day Lighthouse Point Restaurant. Unfortunately, trees on Santa Rosa Island obscured the light beam to ships. The construction of the present lighthouse was begun in 1856, and it was lit January 1, 1859. At night it still shines for sailors 27 miles out at sea, 171 feet tall and with a first-order Fresnel lens. In 1965, the lighthouse was automated, obviating the need for an on-site lighthouse keeper. The Keeper's Quarters now house the navy's Command Display Center, with an exhibit on the lighthouse and the Naval Air Station. The tower is closed to the public, but the lighthouse grounds are open.

PENSACOLA

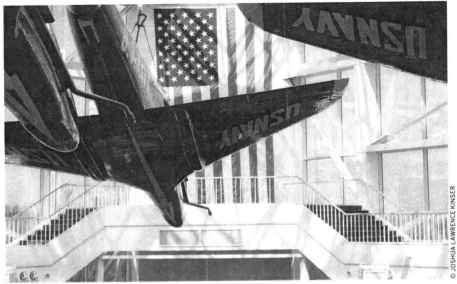

© JOSHUA LAWRENCE KINSER

National Museum of Naval Aviation

The Forts

Accessed through Naval Air Station Pensacola, the historic forts in this area are actually part of the **Gulf Islands National Seashore** (mail: 1801 Gulf Breeze Pkwy., Gulf Breeze, FL 32563, 850/934-2600). The park spans 160 miles from Cat Island, Mississippi, east to the Okaloosa Day Use Area near Fort Walton Beach. The seashore was devastated by Hurricane Ivan, but recovery is now complete.

Fort Barrancas sits on a sandy bluff overlooking the entrance to Pensacola Bay. This site has seen three forts—first an earth-and-log Royal Navy Redoubt in 1763, then a Spanish two-part fort with Bateria de San Antonio at the foot of the bluff and Fort San Carlos de Barrancas above. The American brick-and-mortar Fort Barrancas was mostly completed in 1846, boasting 37 guns. During the Civil War, Confederate forces held Fort Barrancas until 1862. It was rearmed in 1890 and used as a training facility briefly during the Spanish-American War, after which it was disarmed again and used as an observation

and communications post until 1930. Fort Barrancas was deactivated in 1947 and lay unused until it became part of the Gulf Islands National Seashore in 1971. It was entirely restored by 1980 at a cost of $1.2 million. Today, there's a visitors center with exhibits on the history of Pensacola under five flags (1559-1971), with displays of Civil War and coast artillery artifacts. The visitors center shows a 12-minute video on the fort and offers guided tours daily.

The **Fort Barrancas-Advanced Redoubt** (850/455-5167), 700 yards south, was built 1845-1859 to defend the Pensacola Navy Yard from overland infantry assault. It was only manned during the Civil War, after which it was deemed obsolete. Tours are available on Saturday at 11am. The 0.5-mile Trench Trail connects the Advanced Redoubt to the Fort Barrancas Visitor Center.

The largest of the four forts built to defend Pensacola Bay, **Fort Pickens** on Santa Rosa Island sustained serious damage during Hurricane Ivan but is now reopened to the public. All buildings in the historic area were flooded to a depth of several feet and the island experienced major erosion on its south side. The Florida Department of Transportation rebuilt sections of Fort Pickens Road, inland and north of where it used to be.

Construction of the fort was begun in 1829 and completed in 1834; the fort was used until the 1940s. It is said to be the only Southern fort not captured by the Confederacy in the Civil War, and that Geronimo surrendered here in 1886, marking the end of the Apache Wars. The park has a visitors center with a great self-guided tour map of the fort. There are also regularly scheduled ranger tours and a little museum with regular interpretive programs. There is year-round **camping** (850/934-2622, reservations 877/444-6777) in the area on the west end of Santa Rosa Island, as well as the Blackbird Marsh and Dune Nature Trails and a fully repaired fishing pier.

While Fort Pickens is on the western tip of Santa Rosa Island, **Fort McRee** is on a narrow bar of sand on the eastern tip of Perdido Key. Or maybe I should say it used to be there. Once used as the third point of the triangle (with Pickens and Barrancas) by the U.S. Army to defend Pensacola Bay, Fort McRee was built there 1834-1839. It was heavily damaged during the Civil War and then really leveled by hurricanes over the years. It is a great day sailing trip to the fort, where you can usually have the beach and surrounding island all to yourself and wander through the remnants of the fort and Battery 233.

FAMILY-FRIENDLY ATTRACTIONS

There are only so many historic sites a kid can endure before reprehensible behavior sets in. Beyond the area's beaches, there are a couple of fun enticements for young ones. The **Gulf Breeze Zoo** (5701 Gulf Breeze Pkwy., 10 miles east of Gulf Breeze on U.S. 98, 850/932-2229, 9am-4pm daily Jan.-Feb. and Oct.-Dec., 9am-6pm daily Mar-Sept., $14.95 adults, $13.95 seniors, $10.95 children 3-11, children under 3 free) is home to something like 1,400 animals, spread across a 50-acre wildlife preserve. You can view the free-roaming animals from the boardwalk or from the cute red Safari Line train. The train ride is narrated by a guide who points out African wild dogs, giraffes, pygmy hippos, gorillas, and native wildlife. The zoo also has a tranquil Japanese garden, a gift shop, the Jungle Cafe, and Whistlestop Snack Bar.

If you happen to be in town during October, the **Pensacola Interstate Fair** (6655 W. Mobile Hwy., 850/944-4500, $11 12 and over, $5 children 4-11, $5 parking) is vast, with 147 acres of rides and exhibits. It usually takes place the last 11 days of the month. Along with the fair rides and games, the fair always features headline music acts that have included names like Travis Tritt, Switchfoot, and Grand Funk Railroad. Other attractions include livestock, agriculture, and antique car exhibits.

◖ Sam's Fun City

It's fairly small-scale compared to Disney or Busch Gardens, but **Sam's Fun City** (6709 Pensacola Blvd., just south of I-10 on U.S. 29, 850/505-0800, www.samsfuncity.com, 11am-8pm Sun.-Thurs., 11am-10pm Fri. and Sat., weekend hours only during winter, $7-38) is Pensacola's amusement park. There are a bunch of midway-style rides along with go-carts, bumper boats, and miniature golf. It also has a 1,600-square-foot arena for laser tag and a huge game arcade. Sam's recently added **Surf City Water Park** with a wave pool, 15 waterslides, a 1,200-foot-long endless river, spray grounds, water play structures, and kiddie pools. The on-site Bullwinkle's Restaurant is a pleasant, something-for-everyone family restaurant.

Accommodations

UNDER $100

The **Ashton Inn & Suites Pensacola** (4 New Warrington Rd., 850/454-0280, and 910 N. Navy Blvd., 850/455-4561, weekdays $70-85, weekends $80-135) serves the Naval Air Station Pensacola and NTTC Corry Station, and is convenient to the National Museum of Naval Aviation.

My favorite place to stay on Pensacola Beach is the ◖ **Paradise Inn** (21 Via de Luna Dr., 850/932-2319, www.paradiseinn-pb.com, $70-160). Look for the sign with the colorful sun on it. It's easy to miss, but you don't want to do that. The low-rise inn is tucked away among the newer, towering hotels and condos that have sprouted up like sand spurs along the shores of Pensacola Beach. Located right on Santa Rosa Sound and a short walk to the Gulf of Mexico, the Paradise captures the essence of classic Pensacola Beach and the charm of Old Florida. It also offers some of the best waterfront rates in town. The inn's 55 remodeled and renovated rooms are simple but stylish and come equipped with wireless Internet, cable, refrigerators, and microwaves. They surround a casual, fun bar and restaurant run by Renee Mack, who serves a delicious mix of Southern seafood, American fare, and traditional New Orleans-inspired dishes. Renee also runs a very popular and successful catering business, and her food is found at many of the conventions, weddings, and parties around town. The prices are a real treat, with most entrées below $20, but the atmosphere is the clincher. Tables are set upright in the sugar-white sand under a covered pavilion with Santa Rosa Sound just a few feet away. At night, lit tiki torches add to the tropical setting. The inn and restaurant offer a private dock for boaters who want to sail in to dinner or take a break from touring the Intracoastal Waterway for a couple nights' rest. On weekends the Paradise brings in mostly blues, reggae, zydeco, and coastal country musicians for performances on its waterfront stage,

and in recent years has gained a reputation as a favored entertainment venue among locals. They offer room specials on weekdays, so call and check the rates before you arrive.

$100-150

The **Crowne Plaza Pensacola Grand** (200 E. Gregory St., 850/433-3336, $100-150) experienced an extensive renovation in 2005. It has a fully equipped and updated gym on the 2nd floor, an extensive library on the 1st floor, a heated pool, upscale dining in the 1912 Restaurant, and cocktails in the L&L lobby bar. The downtown location is convenient to the historic areas.

OVER $150

On Pensacola Beach, it was a long time after Hurricane Ivan before hotels really rebounded. They're back now, looking better than ever and with many new ones to experience.

Courtyard by Marriott Downtown (700 E. Chase St., 850/439-3330, www.marriott.com, $134-169) opened at the end of 2007, a boon to visitors who wish to enjoy the charm of the downtown area. The five-story hotel features 120 spacious rooms combining comfort and functionality, including high-speed Internet access, large desks, and ergonomic chairs. Amenities include a restaurant for breakfast, large fitness room, and swimming pool with hydrotherapy spa.

You can now find out about the changes in attitudes at the Pensacola Beach latitude at Jimmy Buffet's **Margaritaville Beach Hotel** (165 Fort Pickens Rd., 850/916-9755, www.margaritavillehotel.com, $150-300). The most recent addition to the area, Margaritaville offers very well designed tropical-themed rooms and suites decorated to capture the colors and natural environment of the Gulf of Mexico. All the rooms have free high-speed wireless Internet and flat-screen televisions. The property features an open and airy lobby with nice,

© JOSHUA LAWRENCE KINSER

Margaritaville Beach Hotel on Pensacola Beach

high ceilings and slowly rotating fans that circulate above the Frank and Lola Love Pensacola Café. The café serves breakfast, lunch, and dinner with traditional American breakfast choices and their own spin on the omelet called the Cheese Omelet in Paradise. For lunch it's Cheeseburgers in Paradise and seafood dishes like seafood gumbo and grouper sandwiches. At dinner it's mostly seafood and steaks in Paradise and a great selection of less-expensive salads and sandwiches. Outside the hotel you will find a beautiful pool and a tiki bar. And when you want that Landshark beer and the namesake margarita, you can head over to the Gulf-front Landshark Landing, where you'll find nightly entertainment, volleyball nets, a playground, hammocks tied under palm trees, and a pared-down menu of mostly American food and, you guessed it, Cheeseburgers in Paradise and lots of Jimmy Buffet's Landshark beer on tap.

The **Hilton Pensacola Beach Gulf Front** (12 Via de Luna Dr., 850/916-2999, www.hiltonpensacolabeach.com, $109-259), previously known as the Hilton Garden Inn, is a large beachfront hotel within walking distance of water sports, shopping, dining, and nightlife. Many rooms are Gulf-front rooms and suites with private balconies. At the end of 2007, it added on a new tower with an additional 93 rooms. In addition, the property increased function space from 15,000 square feet to 30,000 square feet to accommodate corporate luncheons, conferences, and wedding receptions. H2O, its signature restaurant featuring Cajun-Asian cuisine, has also nearly doubled in size and now offers a chef's table experience as well as private and semiprivate dining.

Hampton Inn Pensacola Beach (2 Via de Luna Dr., 850/932-6800, www.hamptonpensacolabeach.com, $99-199) has 181 pleasantly outfitted rooms right on the Gulf. The property has a lively tiki bar on the west end of the hotel by the pool, with the waves of the Gulf of Mexico lapping in the background. Ring games and horseshoes are available to entertain visitors, and fun-loving bartenders can whip up any beverage you want, including specialty drinks like the Mojo, Voodoo Juice, or Island Ice Pick.

Another wonderful addition to the area, the historic **Lee House** (400 Bayfront Pkwy., downtown Pensacola, 850/912-8770, www.leehousepensacola.com, $195-245) was damaged by fire in 2001 and knocked down three years later by Hurricane Ivan. It has been resurrected as an upscale bed and breakfast, and the location can hardly be topped. Sitting across from Seville Square Park in the historic district of downtown Pensacola and less than a mile from the foot of the Three Mile Bridge that takes you over to Pensacola Beach, the inn is close to everything you want to experience on your Pensacola visit. The owners, very well known in the area for their culinary success with their local restaurants and catering services Norma's and Norma's-On-The-Go, prepare a wonderful and very large breakfast for guests in the morning. And for those who really love to cook, you can watch Norma prepare the breakfast in the incredible open kitchen. The gathering room in the front of the inn is comfortably upscale with several plush couches and a grand piano taking center stage, where musicians provide a background for guests in the evening. The private and quiet courtyard is a wonderful spot to break for coffee and tea in the afternoon after exploring the historic homes and downtown waterfront surrounding the inn. Each of the eight suites has a unique theme, from the elegant bridal suite with a private jetted tub to the eccentric purple and leopard print room for a zany, fun atmosphere, and a more masculine nautical-themed suite.

For an upscale resort experience on Pensacola Beach, visit the **Portofino Island Resort** (10 Portofino Dr., Bayfront Pkwy., 850/916-5000, www.portofinoisland.com, $380-700). The property comprises five towers with over 300 suites available. Built right at the eastern end of the Gulf Islands National Seashore preserve, which extends seven miles from Pensacola Beach to Navarre Beach, the resort gives you immediate and convenient access to the large stretch of preserved beach with the most beautiful dunes in the area, as well as great flats fishing, kayaking, and boating on Santa Rosa Sound. The resort offers two- and three-bedroom suites, each equipped in an efficiency approach with kitchen, washer and dryer, dining room, private balcony, and living room, offered with 2-, 2.5-, 3-, or 3.5-bathroom floor plans. The two-bedroom suites are spacious with over 1,300 square feet of space. The three-bedroom suites are ultra roomy, offering over 2,000 square feet. Each tower has its own heated pool and spa. Luxurious options include having a private chef come to your suite and cook meals for you or enjoying a massage on your private balcony with sweeping views of the white-sand beaches and Gulf of Mexico stretching out behind the resort.

VACATION RENTALS

Most of the vacation rentals are out on Pensacola Beach. There are a large number of condos available for nightly, weekly, and monthly bookings. Many of the homes for rent that line the Gulf shoreline are large four- and five-bedroom homes. For a more affordable stay, the condos and classic cinder-block homes that dot the residential areas of the beach are a great choice. For vacation rentals on Pensacola beach, contact **Vacation Rentals By Owner** (www.vrbo.com) and search in the Pensacola Beach and Perdido Key areas. If you're interested in staying in the more historic downtown or East Hill areas, check out the rental listings offered by **Pensacola Historic Dream Cottages** (850/232-1266, www.pensacoladreamcottages.com).

Food

DOWNTOWN

Everyone who visits Pensacola has to eat at **The Fish House** (600 S. Barracks St., 850/470-0003, www.goodgrits.com, 11am-midnight Sun.-Thurs., 11am-2am Fri. and Sat., $13-28) at least once. It's been seen on the Travel Channel, in *Food and Wine* magazine, and other leading media (*Wine Spectator* gave its wine list a nod). Just-off-the-docks seafood, sushi, an award-winning chef, and the Fish House Deck Bar—it's all a hit. From a fire pit conversation area and dining tables to an hors d'oeuvres menu and a bandstand with a dance floor, this 3,500 square feet of sun and Gulf breezes offers both local and regional bands serving up live music on Friday and Saturday nights. The Deck's official beer is Landshark.

Very popular with locals, at one of those "disaster café" locations that have seen a lot of restaurants come and go, **The Global Grill** (27 S. Palafox Pl., 850/469-9966, www.dineglobalgrill.com, 5pm-10pm Tues.-Sat., $7-30) offers Pensacola some of its best tapas (actually, some of its only tapas). It's a world-beat approach that includes lamb lollipops with an Israeli couscous cake and sun-dried tomato au jus, or a crab West Indies and avocado martini.

There are a few great, casual pizza joints in town. **HopJacks Pizza Kitchen & Taproom** (10 Palafox Pl., 850/497-6073, www.hopjacks.com, $7-20) offers up plush couches and a stage for local performers. Pizza is the house pride, along with 150 bottled and 36 tap beers. Take a seat inside or grab a slice and head out to the outdoor courtyard for an evening under the stars.

The **Tuscan Oven** (4801 N. 9th Ave., 850/484-6836, www.thetuscanoven.com, 11am-9pm Tues.-Thurs., 11am-10pm Fri.-Sat., $7-20) serves traditional southern Italian thin-crust pizzas prepared in a hardwood-fired oven made of clay, brick, and pumice shipped straight from Italy. The oven and counter bar that wraps around the kitchen are the centerpiece of the cozy dining room. You can chat with the friendly owners and staff while you watch your pizza get prepared and placed in the 500-degree inferno. An outdoor patio for dining or drinking one of the wines from the selective list tops it all off for an extremely enjoyable spot to slice up some pie.

EAST HILL

To the north a bit and east of North Hill Preservation District, East Hill has a couple of my favorite restaurants. **Jerry's Drive-In** (2815 E. Cervantes St., 850/433-9910, 11am-9pm Mon.-Sat., $5-9) offers killer cheeseburgers, onion rings, and fried okra in a comfy diner setting. It's been here since the 1940s, I'm told, and still has a line at lunch (but it's not really a drive-in, it's a walk-in).

J's Pastry (2014 N. 12th Ave., 850/432-4180, 6:30am-6pm Mon.-Sat., 7am-2pm Sun., $2-10) is in the heart of East Hill. J's has been a local favorite for pastries, macaroons, peanut butter bars, and smiley-face cookies since 1946. The small bakery is also well loved for its fresh baked bread, birthday cakes, and tasty apple, cherry, and pecan pies. If you're in town during Mardi Gras, this is the place to get your colorful King's cake. Also along 12th Avenue is **Ozone's Pizza Pub** (1010 N. 12th Ave., 850/433-7336, 11am-midnight Mon.-Sat., 11am-10pm Sun., $10-20), the favorite neighborhood pizza joint. It's a family-friendly place during dinner hours that evolves into a college-aged hangout spot in the evenings. They serve thick-crusted pizza loaded with a generous amount of toppings. Their specialties include an extensive list of meat-centric and vegetarian pizza options, grinders, salads, and pasta dishes, along with a wide selection of beers. **McGuire's Irish Pub** (600 E. Gregory St., 850/433-2849, 11am-2am daily, $10-30) is the Pensacola restaurant everyone knows about. "Irishmen of all nationalities" sign dollar bills

SOMETHING FISHY

It's technically four inches over the Alabama line into Florida's Perdido Key, which took a savage lashing by Hurricane Ivan. You can't keep the irrepressible **Flora-Bama Lounge** (17401 Perdido Key Dr., Perdido Key, 850/492-0611, www.florabama.com) down, though. The longtime beachside roadhouse where fun flows as unchecked as the booze has reopened and been rebuilt to retain its original weathered and ramshackle mystique. The bartenders are famous—and there are 10 bars, along with three stages for bands, volleyball courts, an oyster bar, package store, and sprawling beachside patio.

But that's just the beginning. When it started in 1961, it was a little local bar. It's grown over the years into a huge local bar that looks as if it were built from driftwood and scraps of debris left behind by Hurricane Ivan. It also hosts the international spectacle, the annual **Interstate Mullet Toss,** whereby contestants grip deceased yet slippery fish and throw them as far as they can into the state of Alabama. It's a straight distance competition, but you definitely get style points. Football spiral, underhanded, shot put-style—practice at home with a trout or something to hone your craft.

Several hundred people compete, and nearly 30,000 people turn out to watch the third weekend in April. There's a Ms. Mullet contest, barbecue, crawfish, peel-and-eat shrimp, topless oysters, and a whole lot of cocktails to sweeten the deal. The Flora-Bama has a couple of other annual events of note, one of which is the **Polar Bear Dip** on the morning of January 1, an early morning bar-to-water mad scramble. After a bracing splash in the Gulf (many "bears" leave behind their clothing entirely), revelers go back to the Flora-Bama for some warming black-eyed peas—and if you find a dime in your peas, it's good luck for the whole year.

and staple them to the ceiling, beer is brewed on the premises, the gorgeous wine cellar has a capacity of 8,000 bottles, and you can spend an ungodly sum on a burger (accompanied by caviar and champagne). It's a hard place to describe, really, set in Pensacola's original 1927 Old Firehouse. The steaks are good, and expensive (but it's fitting because all the beef is USDA-certified prime), but it still has a wild-and-woolly Irish pub feel to it. It's vast, with 400 seats and 200 employees, sprawling through a bunch of curio-packed theme rooms. Just go—it'll be fun.

PENSACOLA BEACH

Greatest oyster bar? My personal favorite restaurant on Pensacola Beach? It's **Peg Leg Pete's** (1010 Fort Pickens Rd., 850/932-4139, 11am-10:30pm daily, $8-20), offering some of the best prices on the freshest seafood in Pensacola Beach. The little-known secret around town is that the owner of this fun, family-oriented restaurant also owns Maria's Seafood, the second-largest seafood distributor in town. The rustic and casual, pirate-themed atmosphere of the restaurant and the extensive playground make it a great place for families. The menu features a variety of local favorites and regional classics like grouper sandwiches, crab claws, and a perfect cup of seafood gumbo. Take the stairs down to the ground level and visit the "underwhere?" bar, where they serve cold drinks, raw oysters, and a full menu and feature live music on the weekends.

Flounder's Chowder House (800 Quietwater Beach Rd., 850/932-9081, www.flounderschowderhouse.com, 11am-midnight daily, 11am-2am Fri. and Sat. in summer, $15-24) is a fun, family-oriented place. The fare is lobster, grouper, and shrimp, as well as ribs from the smoker outside. Also on the bay side, **Hemingway's** (400 Quietwater Beach Rd., 850/934-4747, www.hemingwaysislandgrill.com, 11am-9pm daily, $8-33) features an open kitchen and two levels of outdoor deck seating. The menu is island-inspired, with roasted corn and crab chowder, Key West ribs, and shrimp basted with dark rum sauce, and the drinks tend toward the tropical cocktails and beach favorites.

Sidelines (2 Via de Luna Dr., 850/934-3660, www.sidelinespensacola.com, 11am-11pm daily, $7-20) is a fun-loving sports bar and offers a menu with an extensive beer selection and excellent chicken wings, burgers, ribs, and the like. The Caribbean chicken sandwich, smothered in honey barbecue sauce, and the Philly cheesesteak, with a hefty portion of thinly sliced beef, are favorites.

COCKTAILS

The JellyFish Bar (13700 Perdido Key Dr., 850/332-6532) may very well be the perfect spot to end a perfect day on Perdido Key. Specialty cocktails and fine drinks of all varieties take center stage; the signature drink, the jellyfish martini, involves Three Olives-brand vanilla vodka, berry-infused Pucker, and Sprite, and is rimmed with honey that drizzles down inside the glass to complete the jellyfish look. Enjoy the Gulf views on the patio while sippin' on a mojito or Lost Key lemonade.

If you're looking for a local craft beer, head down to the **Pensacola Bay Brewery** (225 E. Zaragoza St., 850/434-3353, www.pbbrew.com, noon-9pm Mon.-Thurs., noon-midnight Fri. and Sat., noon-6pm Sun.) and try one of their 15 seasonal varieties. The brews range from light pilsners to dark oatmeal stouts, and all of them have names that harken back to Pensacola's past. Try a Desoto Berliner Weisse Ale or the Conquistador Dopple Bock, and for a virgin drink, stop in for a delicious Cannonball Rootbeer or their tasty Doubloon Cream Soda. For a behind-the-scenes glimpse into the world of brew mastery, embark on a brewery tour and taste a selection of their finest, chilled cold ones (3:30pm Fri. and Sat.).

Information and Services

Pensacola is located within the **central time zone**. It's that far west. The area code is **850**.

TOURIST INFORMATION

Begin a visit with a stop to the **Pensacola Bay Area Convention & Visitors Bureau information center** (1401 E. Gregory St., at the foot of the Pensacola Bay Bridge, 800/874-1234, www.visitpensacola.com, 8am-5pm Mon.-Fri., 8am-4pm Sat. and Sun.) to pick up maps, brochures, and a copy of the self-guided historic district tours. There's also a convenient **Pensacola Beach Visitors Information Center** (735 Pensacola Beach Blvd., Pensacola Beach, 850/932-1500, 9am-5pm daily).

The main daily newspaper is the **Pensacola News Journal,** and there's a free city magazine called **Pensacola Downtown Crowd** that covers local restaurants and the arts. **Family Sporting Network** is a free and popular paper that covers local sports and can be found on newsstands and business counters throughout the city.

POLICE AND EMERGENCIES

In an emergency, dial 911. If you need medical assistance, **Baptist Hospital** (1000 W. Moreno St., Pensacola, 850/434-4011) has full emergency services, as do **Sacred Heart Hospital** (5152 N. 9th Ave., Pensacola, 850/416-7000) and **Gulf Breeze Hospital** (1110 Gulf Breeze Pkwy., Gulf Breeze, 850/934-2000).

RADIO AND TELEVISION

On the radio, turn to **WUWF 88.1 FM** for NPR, **WTKX 101.5 FM** for straight-ahead rock, **WXBM 102.7** for country radio, and **WCOA 1370 AM** for local talk radio.

For local television programming, **WEAR Channel 3** is the local ABC affiliate, **WKRG Channel 5** is the CBS affiliate out of Mobile-Pensacola, **WALA Channel 10** is the FOX affiliate out of Mobile-Pensacola, **WPMI Channel 15** is the NBC affiliate out of Mobile-Pensacola, **WSRE Channel 23** is PBS, and **WBQP Channel 12** is a local independent.

LAUNDRY SERVICES

If you find yourself in need of coin-op laundry services, try **Dave's** (4124 Mobile Hwy., 850/455-6931) or **9th Avenue Coin Laundry** (6220 N. 9th Ave., 850/471-9224).

Getting There and Around

BY CAR

The major east-west roads in this area are I-10, U.S. 90, and U.S. 98. Running north-south are U.S. 29 and I-110. To get to Pensacola from I-10, you can travel south on Highway 85 into Fort Walton Beach, then west on U.S. 98 to Navarre, then west over Navarre Toll Bridge, and finally west on Highway 399 approximately 20 miles to Pensacola Beach. Or you can go south on I-110 (lots of chain motels along this stretch) or Highway 281, then east on U.S. 98, follow signs to the beaches, and finally drive over Pensacola Beach Toll Bridge into Pensacola Beach. To get to Perdido Key from Pensacola, go west on Highway 292 to Perdido and finally over Perdido Key Bridge onto Perdido Key.

In town, Palafox is the major north-south artery, and Garden Street, which becomes Navy Boulevard on the way to the naval station, runs east-west. The historic district to the waterfront is walkable; for most of the rest of the area you'll need a car. Naval Air Station Pensacola is southwest of the city, and Pensacola Beach is southeast of the city on Santa Rosa Island. Pensacola is connected to Gulf Breeze by the Pensacola Bay Bridge (also called Three Mile Bridge), which in turn is connected to Pensacola Beach by the Bob Sikes Bridge.

BY AIR

Located in Escambia County approximately four miles northeast of downtown Pensacola, **Pensacola International Airport** (2430 Airport Blvd., 850/436-5000) is the biggest airport in northwest Florida, but that's not saying too much. It's not huge, serving more than 100 flights daily from AirTran Airways, American, American Eagle, Continental, Delta, Northwest, and US Airways. Delta has the largest number of direct flights.

Taxis queue up outside the main terminal entrance at baggage claim. Car-rental agencies are inside the main terminal entrance across from baggage claim. **Alamo** (800/327-9633), **Avis** (800/831-2847), **Budget** (800/527-0700), **Dollar** (800/800-4000 domestic, 800/800-6000 international), **Hertz** (800/654-3131), and **National** (800/227-7368) are all on the premises. Enterprise and Thrifty are off-site.

BY BUS AND TRAIN

Amtrak (980 E. Heinberg St., 800/872-7245, www.amtrak.com) has a train station in Pensacola that was still closed at the time of writing due to damaged train tracks from Hurricane Katrina in 2005. **Greyhound Bus Line** (505 W. Burgess Rd., 850/476-4800, www.greyhound.com), however, offers fairly extensive bus service. Such a large military presence usually ensures decent public transportation. There's even a local bus line run by **Escambia County Area Transit** (850/595-3228, www.goecat.com) that includes a University of West Florida (UWF) trolley service and a Pensacola Beach trolley. All in all, it is possible to get around here without a car, but difficult, with some of the more significant attractions inaccessible via public transportation.

THE EMERALD COAST

Some say the emerald color of the water in this area is the result of a blue-green algae. Not true. It's just very clear water, layered over super-reflective white sand in the shallows that produces the green color—the deeper the water, the bluer it gets.

Unified by this eye-catching water color, the beaches of northwest Florida, from Pensacola Beach to the long stretch of the Beaches of South Walton and beyond to the east in Panama City Beach, offer miles of unspoiled natural beauty and a range of options for vacation fun. But they're really different options—this chapter reflects the three distinct draws, each with its own dramatically different character.

First, the **Destin** and **Fort Walton Beach** area in the westernmost part, closest to

Pensacola Beach, is the best-known destination (or Destin-ation, as so many websites pun). Incorporated as recently as 1984, the fishing village of Destin has seen enormous growth as tourism has taken off, with lots of new construction, visitor attractions, and restaurants to lure ever more people. With one of the best geographical locations for fishing on the Gulf Coast, Destin is only 30 miles inland from the 100-Fathom Curve where the best deep-sea fishing for tuna, wahoo, and blue marlin is found. The exciting Destin Seafood Festival and the Destin Fishing Rodeo, both held in October, are testaments to this region's dedication and passion for fishing. It's getting built up, but most of the beachfront is still low-rise (most believe condos will come soon enough, though). Folks visit Destin, Fort Walton Beach,

HIGHLIGHTS

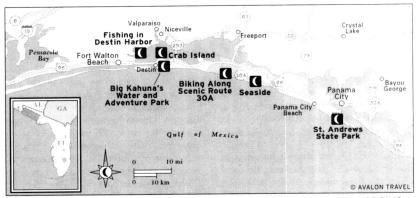

© AVALON TRAVEL

LOOK FOR 【 TO FIND RECOMMENDED SIGHTS, ACTIVITIES, DINING, AND LODGING.

【 **Crab Island:** Rent watercraft to attend the biggest daily impromptu lunch party in Destin on a partially submerged island north of the Destin Bridge (page 31).

【 **Fishing in Destin Harbor:** Offshore, inshore, cobia, sailfish, wahoo—Destin is a serious fishing destination. Arrange a fishing charter to find out why Destin is often called the "World's Luckiest Fishing Village" (page 32).

【 **Big Kahuna's Water and Adventure Park:** If the beach isn't enough to fully occupy the family, head for these 25 acres of waterslides, flumes, tubing, lagoons, wave pools, and more (page 37).

【 **Seaside:** Spend a day exploring this picturesque pastel beach town, featured in the Jim Carrey movie *The Truman Show* (page 43).

【 **Biking Along Scenic Route 30A:** Explore the Beaches of South Walton slowly and under your own power with a bike ride along the 19-mile paved path that follows Scenic 30A (page 46).

【 **St. Andrews State Park:** This park in Panama City, at one point named "the world's best beach" by *Travel Magazine*, offers miles of Gulf-side beach as well as a broad, inviting Grand Lagoon and a 700-acre offshore barrier strip called Shell Island (page 52).

and Okaloosa Island to do some fishing, splash in the emerald-green water, and have a good time with the kids.

The **Beaches of South Walton** region, on the other hand, makes up a 26-mile stretch of shoreline to the east of Destin, containing 14 beach communities. These pristine beaches offer pure, clear, emerald-green water; fine, sugar-white sand; and rare coastal dune lakes; together, these create a unique and varied landscape. It's the first place in the country to receive Blue Wave Environmental Certification from the Clean Beaches Council for all 26 miles of its coastline. Mostly it's private residences in newish, forward-thinking, and ecofriendly planned communities. You won't find a lot of go-cart tracks, mini-marts, or T-shirt shops. Remember that near-perfect town in *The Truman Show*? It was shot here in Seaside—nearly all of the area's towns have this old-fashioned beach retreat style. None of this comes cheap, though. It's pricey to stay in the Beaches of South Walton, but the understated, upscale environment and back-to-basics feel are exceptionally memorable.

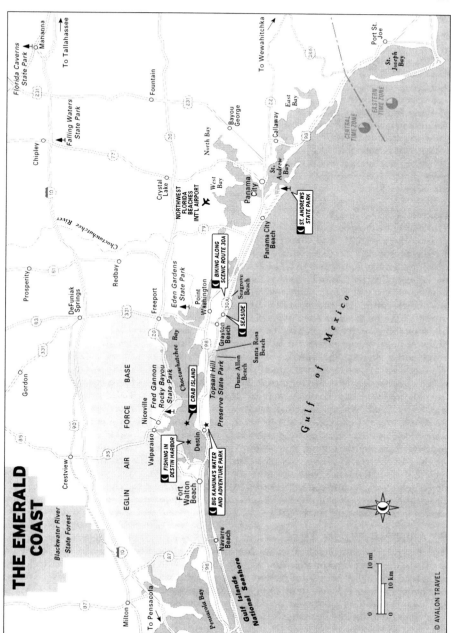

© AVALON TRAVEL

The third section is **Panama City Beach,** about 20 miles farther east. It is best known as the biggest draw along the Gulf Coast of Florida for high school and college spring breakers. If the Beaches of South Walton sounded good, this might not be for you—and vice versa. It's mostly about crowds of people partying and enjoying themselves at the very beautiful beaches, miniature golf courses, video game arcades, and souvenir shops. It's bustling with personal watercraft and parasailers, girls in bikinis, restaurants heavily reliant on deep fryers, and partyers cruising the strip with their car windows down.

HURRICANES

Through Hurricane Ivan in 2004, Hurricane Dennis in July 2005, and then Hurricane Katrina in August 2005 (the costliest and one of the five deadliest hurricanes in U.S. history), the Emerald Coast east from Destin was mostly unaffected. You will see very little evidence of any of these storms, although resulting dredge projects have meant that huge quantities of beach-quality sand have been dragged up for beach re-nourishment efforts. In fact, seven years in the making, the Beaches of South Walton Tourist Development Council completed a large-scale project that restored 26,200 feet of beach over five miles on the west end of Beaches of South Walton, in and around the Sandestin area. More than 75 feet of beach were added in these areas, creating wide, expansive beaches for the public's enjoyment.

The past few years have been an enormous growth period for the area, with new high-rise hotels going up at a rapid clip in Panama City Beach and whole new planned communities erected in the Beaches of South Walton.

PLANNING YOUR TIME

The Forgotten Coast region stretches from Destin in the west to Panama City in the east, a distance of roughly 56 miles. The best way to explore the area is by car, but if you have the luxury of owning a boat you would gain a lot from exploring the Emerald Coast from the water and renting or bringing bikes along

to explore each of the towns. Where to spend most of your time largely depends on what you are interested in doing while in the area. There is a huge diversity in the type of attractions and the cost of accommodations and activities along this stretch of coast. But where to stay? Anglers: Go to Destin or Fort Walton Beach. If you're looking for upscale leisure with coastal beauty all around: Visit the Beaches of South Walton. Spring breakers: Get yourselves to Panama City Beach, and remember to have a designated driver. The latter is worth two days of intensive revelry, three if you have a long attention span. High season along the Panhandle is summer, with rates dropping precipitously in the fall and winter. Spring break is a brief flurry around here in March and April, at its densest in Panama City Beach. Many of the rentals along the 14 communities of the Beaches of South Walton have a minimum stay, some as much as a week during high season. The area could certainly occupy you for that long, with a day trip to Pensacola, another one to visit the amusements in Panama City Beach, and a third to one of the wonderful state parks here. If you're interested in camping and hiking, the area to explore is just east of Destin, where you will find a whole string of great coastal state parks all within a few miles of each other, the best being Topsail Hill Preserve State Park, Grayton Beach State Park, and Henderson State Park. There is an enormous amount of remarkable paddling in Choctawhatchee Bay north of Destin, the freshwater and saltwater lakes that dot the coastline, and in the collection of bays to the north of Panama City. The main road through the area is U.S. 98, which can become quite congested in the busy summer and spring months. Don't miss taking a drive along Highway 30A, which runs south from U.S. 98 through the smaller, upscale communities of Seaside, Blue Mountain Beach, WaterColor, and Rosemary Beach, to name just a few of the picturesque towns along this delightful stretch of coast. Many visitors prefer to rent a bike and pedal along the extensive bike path along Highway 30A. During the summer, spring, and early fall, accommodations along 30A tend to book farther in advance, with the most popular being the cottages at Seaside. Make plans as early as possible if you intend to visit one of these communities during high season. However, in the winter you can often find exceptional prices on some very upscale rooms on this part of the Gulf Coast.

Fort Walton Beach and Destin

Spanish explorer Pánfilo de Narváez landed along the Emerald Coast in 1628 to find himself a drink of water. The Creeks chased him and his men back to the boat, thirst unquenched. There's no telling, really, why up until about 50 years ago a wide swath of the Emerald Coast, from Destin to Panama City, was unsettled sand dunes and quiet green waters. Most of the growth here dates back only a few decades.

Not so of Destin and Fort Walton Beach. Okaloosa County has got roots. In 1830, New England seafarer Leonard Destin fell for the place, the first white man to settle in the area among several local Native American tribes. He lured other New England fishermen with big fish stories, and by 1845 there were 100 white residents, all employed in the fishing business. And Fort Walton Beach was a Civil War campsite, its location chosen because of its protection from the Gulf by the Santa Rosa Sound and Okaloosa Island.

During Prohibition the joint was jumping. "Entrepreneurs" like Al Capone came down to the area to hide out. Mobsters being mobsters, the area was soon dotted with hopping casinos filled with shady characters evading the law up North.

The casinos and mobsters are gone, but what's left is a beloved fishing destination, one

THE EMERALD COAST

© JOSHUA LAWRENCE KINSER

Henderson Beach State Park

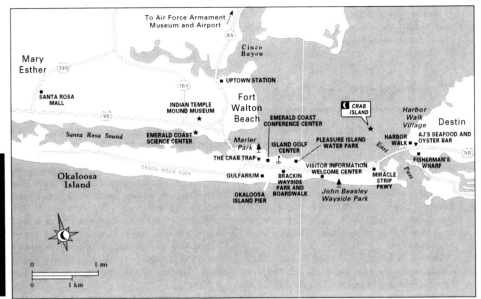

that boasts five saltwater world records. It looks the part: Destin and Fort Walton Beach were the shooting location for *Jaws II,* both admirably portraying charming seaside resort towns.

SPORTS AND RECREATION
Beaches

There are 24 miles of beach—the sand a shockingly fine, white quartz that somehow made its way here down 130 miles of the Appalachian River, the water a brilliant jewel green. Nearly 60 percent of the beach around here is preserved in perpetuity, or at least for a long, long time. There are five beachfront parks and 12 beach access ways along the Destin, Fort Walton Beach, and Okaloosa Island shoreline.

One of the best is the 208-acre **Henderson Beach State Park** (17000 Emerald Coast Pkwy., east of the city of Destin on U.S. 98, 850/837-7550, for camping call 800/326-3521 or visit www.reserveamerica.com, 8am-sundown daily, $4/vehicle with single occupant, $6/vehicle with up to 8 passengers, $2 pedestrian or cyclist, $30 camping), which has 6,000

feet of shoreline. There's urban sprawl off to the west in Destin; in fact, the beach's entrance is just across the street from a Walmart Supercenter. Once out on the coastal dunes you'd never know it—sea oats anchor the soft sand in the dunes, while the ocean's salt spray and wind cause the rosemary, magnolias, and scrub oak to grow low and horizontal, their limbs bent shoreward. During the fall the beach is dotted with colorful wildflowers—blanket flower and beach morning glory carpeting the clean sand.

At Henderson you can swim, surf fish, picnic, bike, in-line skate, walk the 0.75-mile nature trail, or camp (the campground has 60 full-facility campsites for tents or RVs). Colored flags indicate the wave and swimming conditions—red flag means "knee deep is too deep" as there is high potential for rip currents to form, and double red flag means the water is closed for swimming.

James Lee County Park (3510 Scenic U.S. 98, Destin, 8am-sundown daily, free parking) is another good beach, right at the Walton/

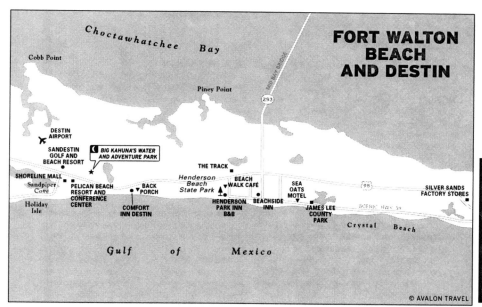

FORT WALTON BEACH AND DESTIN

Choctawhatchee Bay

Cobb Point

Piney Point

293

DESTIN AIRPORT

SANDESTIN GOLF AND BEACH RESORT

BIG KAHUNA'S WATER AND ADVENTURE PARK

THE TRACK

SHORELINE MALL

Sandpiper Cove

PELICAN BEACH RESORT AND CONFERENCE CENTER

BACK PORCH

Henderson Beach State Park

BEACH WALK CAFE

Holiday Isle

COMFORT INN DESTIN

HENDERSON PARK INN B&B

BEACHSIDE INN

SEA OATS MOTEL

JAMES LEE COUNTY PARK

98

SILVER SANDS FACTORY STORES

SCENIC HWY 98

Crystal Beach

Gulf of Mexico

© AVALON TRAVEL

THE EMERALD COAST

Okaloosa County line. This park has three pavilions, 41 picnic tables, nine dune walkovers, a playground, restrooms with changing rooms, and 166 parking spaces. It's a popular beach for families, with the water shallow and clear and the Crab Trap restaurant in the middle of the beach's parking lot.

Okaloosa Island has a series of beaches, really contiguous—first, the **John Beasley Wayside Park** (U.S. 98, Okaloosa Island, 1.2 miles east of Fort Walton Beach, 850/546-0342) is on the bay side of the barrier island just yards from the Okaloosa Boardwalk (an entertainment complex with clubs and restaurants). John Beasley has restrooms, picnic tables, showers, changing rooms, vending machines, and lifeguards. It has fishing for trout and reds, snorkeling activity, and even a little surfing. The same can be said of the adjacent **Brackin Wayside Park and Boardwalk** (U.S. 98, Okaloosa Island, 1 mile east of Fort Walton Beach, 850/651-7131), which has several pavilions, 41 picnic tables, restrooms with changing rooms, a children's playground, dune walkovers to the beach, lots

of parking, and fierce beach volleyball during the warmer months.

Crab Island

You've got an appointment to keep. To get there, you need something that floats—maybe a pontoon boat, or a glass-bottom boat, or a fishing boat, or even a Wave Runner. You can shop at **Boogies Watersports** (16 Harbor Blvd., www.boogieswatersports.com, 850/654-4497) to pick up a rental that suits your budget, skill level, and personal sense of style. But you're in a hurry. It's a lunch date.

You're going to need directions, but any local can tell you how to get to Crab Island. North of the Destin Bridge, it used to be two islands in the middle of nowhere, made of sand dredged by the U.S. Army Corps of Engineers from East Pass. It used to even be a real island with sea grass, shrubs, and seabirds. But now it's submerged a few feet and only surfaces at low tide. But it's where people congregate for a lunchtime bash. Boats pile up out there and people jump off into the three-foot shallows, eating,

BEACH BASICS

So that your day at the beach can be an, um, day at the beach, keep a few things in mind.

BEACH HUSBANDRY

Bare coastal dunes are vulnerable to destruction by the same forces that form them: wind and waves. Dunes are built when sand blows up through beachside plant life and is trapped, creating ever-taller mounds. These mounds in turn protect the shore during storms by washing back out to sea and decreasing the energy of the storm waves. For these reasons, do not trample, pick, spindle, or mutilate any beachside plant life (like the sea oats). In fact, along public beach accesses, always use the **boardwalks and raised walkways** rather than tramping through the sand.

Sea turtles nest on the Gulf beaches of Okaloosa County April-November. Recent hurricane seasons have wrought havoc on these already threatened and endangered species. Again, no spindling (it's illegal to disturb a nest or harm a turtle in any way), or even taunting. Never crowd around a turtle nest, don't impede a turtle's progress toward the water, and don't shine lights on the beaches at night if possible.

This area's beaches are all **clothing-required.** Navarre Beach used to have a lot of nude sunbathers, but federal agents have cracked down on the depravity and lawlessness that comes of lying nude on a beach towel. Be advised. Also, beaches in this area **prohibit pets,** and that goes double for nude pets. If you see animals on the beach, they probably belong to residents who have gotten special beach pet permits, available only to locals.

BEACH SAFETY

Jellyfish are common to Gulf beaches. Not the big, terrifying Man O' War types, but the local species' sting can still be pretty fierce. Shuffle your feet in the water to alert nearby jellyfish to your presence. In the event that you do get stung, the experts say ammonia poured on the sting relieves the pain, as does meat tenderizer and toothpaste. (Who figures these things out—is someone getting stung and then applying poultices of household products just in the name of science?—"Preparation H, yes. Mr. Clean, no.")

Rip currents occur in any type of weather. If caught in a rip current, swim parallel to the shore until the current weakens and you can swim in.

And although shark attacks in these waters are very infrequent, there are ways to further minimize your chances of a **shark encounter.** You're more vulnerable if you're swimming alone, and if you swim far from shore. Sharks are most active at dusk, when they have a competitive sensory advantage. They tend to hang out in areas between sandbars or steep drop-offs—use caution when swimming in these areas. As you know, sharks smell blood—if you have a wound, if you are menstruating, or if nearby fisherfolk are cleaning fish or throwing out bait, think about postponing a swim. And remove shiny jewelry before you go in—its reflective glinting looks like the sheen of fish scales to a hungry predator.

Use **sunscreen,** and lots of it. Experts say that an average-sized person should use about two tablespoons per application.

chatting, and drinking. Sometimes there's even live music on the back of a boat or floating vendors serving food and drinks (often an ice-cream guy) to all the folks gathered there.

◖ Fishing in Destin Harbor

About 30 miles offshore (only 10 miles from Destin's East Pass), the Gulf of Mexico turns from emerald green to deep blue. It's at this point, called the 100-Fathom Curve, where you're in deep, deep water all of a sudden. This deep-water curve is closer to Destin than to any other spot in Florida, meaning a fishing charter from Destin is the quickest way out to deep water. And it's a lucky thing, because these waters are churning with fish. In the spring there's the migration of mighty cobia (you can sight fish for these) and in May come the kingfish (inshore troll). People bottom fish for grouper, red snapper, triggerfish, and amberjack year-round. In summer, when the waters warm up, it's serious marlin and sailfish (offshore troll) and wahoo and tuna (inshore troll). Destin bills itself, so to speak, as the Billfish Capital of the World. The best I can figure, based on conversation with sometimes-taciturn fisher types, billfish is a tuna-like fish species similar to marlin, sailfish, and spearfish—those fish with the big, sword-like bill. Destin is also known by some as the "World's Luckiest Fishing Village," because its waters harbor four times more types of fresh fish per season than any other Florida destination except for Key West. Supposedly, during any given season there are 20 edible species of gamefish to be found in local waters.

So you have to come here and fish. Offshore, bottom, inshore, or even surf-casting—there are lots of people around here with enormous experience willing to take you out on a saltwater charter or just hook you up with gear. In addition, the area's rivers offer freshwater fishing for catfish, bass, and bream. And many restaurants in the area are willing to cook up your fresh catch.

The price of a private charter averages $150-165 per hour, for up to six people. Many boats only accommodate six people, so make clear how many people are in your party. You can also sign up for a group charter, pooling with other people who are looking to go out (prices are the same, you just split it between all the people on the boat). Obviously, you have to find others who are simpatico, in terms of what they're fishing for and how long they want to be out. **Destin Charter Service** (Fisherman's Wharf, 850/837-1995) is one-stop shopping, with access to 40 of Destin's best charter boats (there are more than 100 vessels for hire around here). These boats offer year-round fishing trips for individuals or groups, from four-hour trips to overnights, either on the Gulf or the bay side. **Harborwalk Fishing Charters** (next to Lucky Snapper off U.S. 98, 10 Harbor Blvd., 850/837-2343, www.harborwalkfishing.com, $105/person for 4 hours, $165/person for 6 hours—it's customary to tip 15 percent) is

another well-regarded local charter company. Staff will clean, fillet, and bag your catch at trip's end. **Captain John Holley** (next to Lucky Snapper off U.S. 98, 797 Pine St, 850/837-4946, www.catchbigmarlin.com) specializes in big fish. He has a number of marlin, cobia, and kingfish tournament wins to his credit and has been involved in many of the local billfish tournaments (they're tag and release). He was the Destin Rodeo Sportfishing Captain of the Year for nine consecutive years. Prices vary by the type of fish: cobia $1,000 full day, $600 half; trolling and live bait fishing for marlin, tuna, wahoo, mahimahi, and king mackerel $150 per hour; and bottom fishing for amberjack and grouper $150 per hour.

If you just feel like finding your own boat and giving it a go, **Gilligan's Water Sports** (Destin Harbor, 530 Harbor Blvd., 850/650-9000, www.gilligansofdestin.com) rents pontoon boats for reasonable prices ($150-400), good for snorkeling, fishing, or just tooling around. You can also head out into the Blackwater, Shoal, or Yellow Rivers in search of bass, bream, and catfish.

No boat is required to fish from the **Okaloosa Island Fishing Pier** (850/244-1023, 24 hours daily, $7.50 adults, $4.50 children 6-12, no license necessary). It's a 1,261-foot pier, lighted at night, with rod holders and benches built into it. You'll catch all kinds of things (including big mahimahi). You can also cast from the area's finger jetties, sandy shores, and the 3,000-foot **Destin Bridge Catwalk** to hook speckled trout, white snapper, and redfish. And there are stocked ponds in the area, such as the 350-acre **Hurricane Lake** in Blackwater River State Park, filled with channel catfish, largemouth bass, bluegill, and shellcracker.

When you want to find out what is biting and where, visit www.gulfcoastangling.com, then plan your fishing accordingly.

Shelling and Diving

The beaches are uniformly fine white sand, and compared to the beaches to the south there are very few shells in sight. So how can the Emerald Coast be ranked as a top shelling destination?

Destin is spoiled for choice with an abundance of beautiful and diverse beaches.

They're offshore—you have to dive for them. Giant sandbars about a mile from shore and a natural coral-encrusted limestone outcropping (the pre-ice age shoreline) three miles out act as natural shovels to collect perfectly formed shells—pastel lion's paws, true tulips, huge queen helmets, and Florida's signature shell, the horse conchs, are there for the picking.

The center of much of this shelling mania is **Sand Dollar City,** an artificial reef complex the county put together about a mile out. It's got six patch reefs placed in a hexagonal pattern around a single center point, the sunken 1941 tugboat called the *Mohawk Chief.* The whole area is a fish and shellfish haven, and by extension, a shelling bonanza. **Timber Hole** is another hot spot of shelling and intriguing marinelife observation (sea squirts, four-foot basket sponges, aqua and purple sea whips). It has a natural limestone reef 6-18 feet high and 110 feet deep, as well as sunken planes, ships, and a railroad car. There are loads of natural reefs in this area, for shelling, diving, and fishing; **Amberjack Rocks** is one of

the area's largest reef systems, within three miles of Destin Pass. About 80 feet deep, it is known for shelling as well as spearfishing for black snapper and amberjack. **Long Reef** features staircase ledges and is known for lobsters and shells. The area also has intriguing wrecks to explore—an air force barge, a Liberty ship, Butler's Barge, and the rubble of the Destin Bridge. Divers here often enjoy 40-100 feet of visibility.

For safety reasons, all divers must display a free-flying, 12- by 12-inch flag with a white diagonal stripe on a red background—the diver-down flag—in the area in which the dive occurs. Divers should try to stay within 100 feet of the flag, and the flag and diver should never be in areas that might constitute a navigational hazard.

Emerald Coast Scuba (503-B Harbor Blvd., Destin, 850/837-0955, www.divedestin.com) provides scuba instruction and charters. Many other dive shops offer theme excursions like spearfishing, deep sea, shell, and lobster, with certification classes. They will also take you out

EAST PASS

Originally, the Gulf of Mexico and the Destin Harbor did not connect to the Choctawhatchee Bay in this area, which posed some navigational challenges to the local fishing fleet and some flooding danger to the settlements as well. In 1926, three local, stalwart families took it upon themselves to change that. The Destins, the Marlers, and the Melvins grabbed a bunch of shovels and started digging by hand, making a two-foot-wide ditch across Okaloosa Island. Within two hours, supposedly, the trench was over 100 yards wide. A torrent of water rushed in, creating what is now East Pass. In 1935 the East Pass Bridge was built. To this day, the U.S. Army Corps of Engineers keeps close tabs on the pass, dredging it every two years or so (more in hurricane years) to ensure the water's deep enough for boats to move safely through it.

The East Pass is the only waterway connecting the Choctawhatchee Bay to the Gulf of Mexico for 60 miles in either direction (Pensacola to the west and Panama City to the east each have waterways that connect the bay with the Gulf). The East Pass is the lifeblood of the Destin fishing fleet—without it, the town would surely not be the angler's paradise that draws fisherfolk from around the world. All because of a few shovels.

snorkeling from their boats. If you just want to snorkel on your own, you can do so from the beach at **Destin Jetties** or from the **Old Crystal Beach Pier.**

Golf

Emerald-green waters mirrored by emerald-green golf courses. There are 1,080 holes of golf in these parts, many of the courses designed by some of the world's best architects: Robert Cupp of Jack Nicklaus fame, or Finger, or Dye, or Fazio. Many of these courses utilize the area's lush natural beauty and surrounding waterways, with contrasts of woods and wetlands, for challenging and memorably beautiful play.

The 18-hole **Regatta Bay Golf Club** (465 Regatta Bay Blvd., Destin, 850/337-8080, www.regattabay.com, $59-129, par 72, 6,864 yards, course rating 73.8, slope 148) was designed by Robert Walker, winding along the shore of Choctawhatchee Bay and carved through wetlands and protected nature preserves. Another popular one, the creation of Fred Couples and Gene Bates, **Kelly Plantation Golf Club** (307 Kelly Plantation Dr., Destin, 850/650-7600, www.kellyplantationgolf.com, $60-140, par 72, 7,099 yards, course rating 74.2, slope 146) utilizes the Choctawhatchee Bay as well, nestled along its southern edge with rolling greens and beautiful fairways.

Acclaimed by *Golfweek* as one of the 50 Most Distinctive Development Courses in the Southeast, **Emerald Bay** (40001 Emerald Coast Pkwy., Destin, 850/837-5197, $35-105, par 72, 6,802 yards, course rating 73.1, slope 135) was designed by nationally recognized architect Robert Cupp. He said of the course, "There is no signature hole, it is—instead—a signature golf course."

At **Indian Bayou Golf and Country Club** (1 Country Club Dr. E., Destin, 850/837-6191, www.indianbayougolf.com, $39-75, par 72, 7,000 yards, course rating 74, slope 132-142) there's an assortment of Earl Stone-designed nines, the Choctaw, Seminole, and Creek, which can be played in any 18-hole combination. The Creek course, the newest, has lots of water that comes into play; the Choctaw is heavily wooded; and the Seminole has wide fairways and large greens.

Also situated on the banks of Choctawhatchee Bay, **Shalimar Pointe Golf and Country Club** (302 Country Club Rd., Shalimar, 850/651-4300, $29-59, par 72, 6,765 yards, course rating 72.9, slope 125) is a Finger/Dye-designed course that *Links* magazine accused of having "Two of the Hardest Holes on the Emerald Coast," the 11th and 17th. It is bordered by rolling white dunes and dense hammocks of pine, oak, and magnolia.

Shalimar Pointe has been host to The Emerald Coast Tour.

Beyond these, there's **Shoal River Country Club, Fort Walton Beach Municipal Course,** the two courses at **Eglin Air Force Base** (available only with government ID), and the world-class courses at Sandestin.

SIGHTS
Museums

Located near Eglin Air Force Base's main gate, the **Air Force Armament Museum** (Hwy. 85 and Hwy. 189, seven miles north of Fort Walton Beach, 850/651-1808, 9:30am-4:30pm Mon.-Sat., admission free) is the only facility in the United States dedicated to the display of air force armament. You'll see thousands of weapons, an educational film called *Arming the Air Force,* and photography exhibits in addition to 25 cool reconnaissance, fighter, and bomber planes. There's a B-17 Flying Fortress, an F-4 Phantom II jet, and an SR-71 Blackbird Spy Plane. The museum spans four wars in its scope—World War II, Korea, Vietnam, and Persian Gulf. Kids love the fighter cockpit simulator.

The Fort Walton Beach community has a rich Native American past, settled by a number of prehistoric tribes as far back as 12,000 BC. The **Indian Temple Mound Museum and Park** (139 Miracle Strip Pkwy. SE, Fort Walton Beach, 850/833-9595, 10am-4:30pm Mon.-Sat. June-Aug., noon-4:30pm Mon.-Fri., 10am-4:30pm Sat. Sept.-May, $5.30 adults, $4.77 seniors, $3.18 children 4-17, children 3 and under free) provides a peek into the area's Native American history, with a thoughtfully assembled collection of southeastern Indian ceramic artifacts and an Indian Mound Temple that dates to AD 1400 and originally served as a religious and civic center.

It was the first schoolhouse constructed for the children of Camp Walton, later to be known as Fort Walton Beach. **Camp Walton Schoolhouse Museum** (127 Miracle Strip Pkwy. SE, Fort Walton Beach, 850/833-9595, noon-4pm Mon.-Sat., $5.30 adults, $4.77 seniors, $3.18 children 4-17, children 3 and under free) was built of native pine and oak, and when it opened in 1912 there were 15 students and one teacher. It was restored in the early 1970s and opened as an educational museum in 1976. These days, it's mostly for the benefit of local school groups, but it still makes a sweet nostalgic look at a past most of us never knew.

Family-Friendly Attractions

A good example of the compelling science museums for kids that seem to be popping up in every town these days is the **Emerald Coast Science Center** (139 Brooks St., Fort Walton Beach, 850/664-1261, www.ecscience.org, 9am-6pm Mon.-Sat., noon-4pm Sun., $5.75 adults, $4.75 seniors, $3.75 children 3-17, children 2 and under free), which has an interesting section devoted to color and light. You can fly and land a model airplane in a mini air tunnel, or noodle with a laser spirograph or a Van de Graff generator (you know, that orb that makes your hair stand on end). There's also a nature part to the museum, with tarantulas and giant millipedes, and a human body section with presentations about the digestive system, the five senses, and the skeleton.

Opened in 1955, **Gulfarium** (1010 Miracle Strip Pkwy., Fort Walton Beach, 850/243-9046, 9am-4:30pm daily, closes earlier seasonally, $19.95 adults, $18.95 seniors, $11.95 children 3-11, children 2 and under free) was one of the country's original marine parks. Like a mini Sea World, it hosts Atlantic bottlenose dolphins, California sea lions, Peruvian penguins, Ridley turtles, and lots of Gulf-focused educational marine exhibits. The Gulfarium was closed for quite a while after the hurricane season of 2004, but the closure ultimately resulted in even better dolphin shows with high jumps and soccer games, and a sweet sea lion show (they're not bad Frisbee players, considering the lack of opposable thumbs and all). For a fairly hefty fee ($150), guests can also have one-on-one interactions with the dolphins. The Gulfarium also sponsors the Dolphin Project, which focuses on interaction between dolphins and children with disabilities (like autism).

◖ BIG KAHUNA'S WATER AND ADVENTURE PARK

Even adults get a little wide-eyed when they begin describing **Big Kahuna's Water and Adventure Park** (1007 U.S. 98 E., Destin, 850/837-4016, www.bigkahunas.com, 10am-6pm all summer, water park closed in winter and adventure park with weekend hours only, $38 adults, $30 children and seniors, children 2 and under free), with more than 40 water attractions and an adventure park spread over 25 acres. Clad in your bathing suit and a smile, you can wind through caves and waterfalls (the Tiagra Falls pumps 30,000 gallons of water per minute over 250 feet of mountain granite rock). There are three rivers, speed slides, body flumes, white-water tubing, leisurely lagoons, two wave pools, four children's areas with kid-sized slides and variable-depth pools, and other exciting wet-and-wild attractions for kids of all ages. Then once you dry off, visit the attached Adventure Park attractions (be aware, it's a separate ticket price, and a steep one—it's cheaper if you get the combined all-day pass for, gulp, $57). There are 54 holes of miniature golf, a go-cart raceway, a bunch of other rides, and an arcade.

ENTERTAINMENT AND EVENTS
The Arts
The attractions on the Emerald Coast are mostly outdoors, where the sun, sand, and fish are. While art is not the largest draw for the Emerald Coast, it doesn't disappoint. The **Northwest Florida Ballet** (310 Perry Ave SE, Fort Walton Beach, 850/664-7787) is the longest-running arts organization in northwest Florida, producing full-length semiprofessional ballets in a number of local venues, including summer ballet in the park and the requisite holiday performance of *The Nutcracker*. **Stage Crafters Community Theatre** (40 Robinwood Dr. SW, Fort Walton Beach, 850/243-1101, www.stagecrafters.com, 7:30pm, 2pm matinees, $20 musicals, $15 non-musicals) is a small community troupe that puts on plays like the familiar *Godspell* and the

unfamiliar *Meshuggah-Nuns*. The **Northwest Florida State College's Mattie Kelly Fine and Performing Arts Center** (100 College Blvd., Niceville, 850/729-6000, www.mattiekellyartscenter.org) stages community plays and hosts Broadway touring acts and other big ticket performers in its large 1,650-seat main theater, but also hosts dance, opera, the Northwest Florida Symphony Orchestra, and other arts events.

In visual arts, the **Arts & Design Society** (17 First St. SE, Fort Walton Beach, 850/244-1271, www.artdesignsociety.org), founded in 1956 by a group of local artists, is more of a community art outreach, with classes, lectures, and children's programs, but it also hosts monthly local, regional, and national exhibits that are worth checking out.

Festivals
In the Destin area, there are annual events like the Spring Splash, the Billy Bowlegs Festival, the Sandestin Wine Festival, and the Christmas Boat Parade—but the biggest of them all is the monthlong **Destin Fishing Rodeo** in October. There are 30 different categories of prizes, with all saltwater game fish eligible—so you'll see people fishing all over the place with a vengeance. There's a more focused, single-species event in March and April with the annual Cobia Tournaments.

NIGHTLIFE
Destin and Fort Walton Beach can get lively, then it's quiet again to the east in the Beaches of South Walton area; still farther east in Panama City Beach it gets hopping again. Here, head dockside to **AJ's Club Bimini** (on the Destin Harbor, 0.25 mile east of the Destin Bridge, 116 Harbor Blvd., 850/837-1913, 11am-4am daily) for a Bimini Bash, a powerful concoction of cranberry, orange, and pineapple juices with a five-rum roundhouse punch. Then try out one of the theme nights at the sprawling **Nightown** (140 Palmetto St., Destin, 850/837-6448, www.nightown.com) and groove with the DJ. Or you could just stop in for a margarita at **Pepito's** (757 Harbor Blvd., Destin,

850/650-7734, until 4am daily), in front of the Destin Cinemas, or get crazy on the dance floor at **Harry T's** (46 Harbor Blvd., Destin, 850/654-4800, 11am-11pm daily), which recently moved to the Harbor Walk village. Opened by a big top trapeze artist, Harry T's is adorned with circus memorabilia, including a stuffed giraffe, and treasures from the sunken luxury liner *Thracia.* Then warm up with a few scales, because crowd participation is required at the dueling piano bar of **Howl at the Moon** (The Boardwalk, Okaloosa Island, 850/301-0111).

SHOPPING

Silver Sands Factory Stores (10562 Emerald Coast Pkwy. W, on U.S. 98, 8 miles east of Destin, near Sandestin Golf & Beach Resort, Destin, 850/654-9771, www.silversandsoutlet. com, 10am-9pm Mon.-Sat., 10am-6pm Sun.) is supposedly the nation's largest designer outlet center. And it keeps growing. Think Off Saks Fifth Avenue, Ann Taylor, Polo Ralph Lauren, Dooney & Bourke, Tommy Hilfiger, Ellen Tracy, Adrienne Vittadini, Banana Republic, Liz Claiborne, and the like. If shoes are your thing: Nine West Outlet, Famous Footwear, Liz Claiborne Shoes, Kenneth Cole, and Cole Haan. There are more than 100 designer outlet stores within 450,000 square feet of retail space, drawing something like six million shoppers annually.

ACCOMMODATIONS

Under $100

Because of spring break maniacs, most of the hotels around here don't rent to people under 25 (unless they're with an "adult"). One of the good and bad things about the Destin area is that there aren't too many big hotels right on the beach. Most lodgings are just a bit of a drive. If you are looking for a quiet, independently owned place right at water's edge, try **Sea Oats Motel** (3420 Old U.S. 98 E., Destin, 850/837-6655, $85-160), which is a long, low-slung motel right on the sand, offering condo rentals as well.

If you're willing to hop in the car or on a bike to hit sand, there's the **Beachside Inn** (2931 Scenic U.S. 98, Destin, 850/650-9099, $85-180), with brightly colored rooms in a modest-sized low-rise hotel. **Comfort Inn Destin** (19001 Emerald Coast Pkwy., Destin, 850/654-8611, $85-145) is fairly new and pretty deluxe for a Comfort Inn—no offense. It's got 100 rooms, nicely appointed, and two pools (one indoors).

$100-150

The **Best Western Summerplace Inn** (14047 Emerald Coast Pkwy., Destin, 850/650-8003, $110-150) is in the heart of Destin, a quick drive to public beach access. There's a decent complimentary continental breakfast, indoor and outdoor pools with a big whirlpool, and free high-speed Internet access.

Over $150

There are plenty of condos right on the beach, many only renting by the week in high season. The **Pelican Beach Resort and Conference Center** (1002 U.S. 98 E., Destin, 888/654-1425, $150-300, two-night minimum much of the year) is a big, imposing cube. **Hidden Dunes Beach and Tennis Resort** (9815 U.S. 98 W., Destin, 850/654-1325, $130-600) has several ways to go, from a unit in a 20-story tower at water's edge, to luxurious three- and four-bedroom villas overlooking the private Hidden Dunes lake, to Carolina-style cottages with private screened porches, nestled in a wooded landscape. Farther east, into the Beaches of South Walton town of Seascape, the **Majestic Sun** (1160 Old U.S. 98, Destin, 850/837-8264, $110-375) is a huge condo tower with beautiful pools, tennis, and golf, all just across the street from the beach. **Sandpiper Cove** (775 Gulfshore Dr., Destin, 855/837-9121, www.sandpipercove.com, $170-320) is pretty much a Destin landmark, with a 43-acre landscaped property that has its own 1,100 feet of beach. These are individually owned (and decorated) condo units, so look at the pictures before deciding what's right for you. The property has five swimming pools and three outdoor hot tubs.

My favorite place to stay in the area is the **Henderson Park Inn Bed & Breakfast** (2700

THE EMERALD COAST

Henderson Park Inn Bed & Breakfast

Scenic U.S. 98, 866/398-4432, www.hendersonparkinn.com, $179-689), northwest Florida's only beachside bed-and-breakfast. Beyond the inn's lovely setting adjacent to the 208-acre Henderson Beach State Park, travelers are spoiled with tidbits like complimentary breakfast and lunch, nightly sunset glasses of wine and beer, an arrival wine and fruit assortment, evening turndown service with sweets, and a stocked kitchen pantry, all included in the room price. Guests also get complimentary use of water-sports equipment, high-speed Internet access, and beach service with chair and umbrella setup.

Vacation Rentals

If you want to rent a beach cottage or luxurious condominium, **Newman-Dailey Resort Properties** (12815 U.S. 98 W, Ste. 100, Destin, 850/837-1071 or 800/225-7652, www.destinvacation.com) is a well-regarded property management and vacation rental company that's been in the area for the past 22 years. The website offers virtual tours of properties.

FOOD

The restaurants of Destin, Fort Walton Beach, and Okaloosa Island tend to focus on fish, with lots of casual oyster bars and fish shacks. There are upscale spots around, but the best places are the Southern-style casual seafood joints.

Breakfast

Start your day, and your visit, at the **Donut Hole** (635 U.S. 98 E., Destin, 850/837-8824, 6am-10pm daily, $4-12). It's breakfast all day, with sturdy baked goods and nice people.

Casual

The **C Back Porch** (1740 Old U.S. 98 E., Destin, 850/837-2022, 11am-9pm daily, $10-25) is a fun, cedar-shingled seafood shack, an ideal place to try your first char-grilled amberjack. The view is great—you won't mind waiting because you can hang out right on the beach while they ready a table. Also, it's a notable surf spot, so you can watch surfers paddling out hopefully to the break.

The tiki-topped **AJ's Seafood and Oyster**

Bar (0.25 mile east of the Destin Bridge, Destin, 850/837-1913, 10am-11pm daily, 10am-9:30pm in the off-season, no reservations, $9-21) is another longtime beachside visitor favorite. Overlooking Destin Harbor, AJ's Club Bimini is the place to see the sunset over a plate of Oysters AJ (oysters baked with jalapeños, Monterey jack, and bacon). AJ's charter fleet offers daily trips into shallow or deep waters to hunt for grouper, amberjack, and wahoo—the kitchen will cook your catch straight off the line. Try the fried fish sandwiches or the shrimp po'boy.

Don't like fish? **Fudpucker's Beachside Bar & Grill** (20001 Emerald Coast Pkwy., Destin, 850/654-4200, 1318 Miracle Strip Pkwy., Okaloosa Island, Fort Walton Beach, 850/243-3833, www.fudtv.com, 11am-10pm daily, $8-20) is the place for burgers, drinks on the deck, and some of the best bands on the beach.

In Fort Walton Beach, **The Crab Trap** (1450 Miracle Strip Pkwy., Okaloosa Island Boardwalk, Fort Walton Beach, 850/301-0959, 11am-10pm daily, $7-25), nestled in the beautiful James Lee County Park and overlooking the water, graciously accommodates the sand between your toes and your unmistakable whiff of suntan oil. Grouper, tuna, and amberjack are the freshest catches, with lots of fried seafood and all-you-can-eat snow-crab legs (they're not from around here, though). It's casual, but not as casual as the nearby **Angler's Beachside Grill and Sports Bar** (1030 Miracle Strip Pkwy., Okaloosa Island Boardwalk, Fort Walton Beach, 850/796-0260, www.anglersgrill.com, 11am-9pm Mon.-Thurs., 11am-10pm Fri.-Sat., 10am-2pm Sun. for brunch, $7-20). You can eat right on the boardwalk or inside with all the games on big TVs.

Fine Dining

Some of the best food in the area is to be had from Chef John Sallman at the ❰ **Beach Walk Café** (Henderson Park Inn, 2700 U.S. 98 E., Destin, 850/650-7100, www.beachwalkhendersonpark.com, 5:45pm-11pm daily, $26-54). There is pecan-crusted grouper served over roasted and crisped potato cakes, and classic smoked-gouda shrimp and grits, just to name a few. It's one of the best fine-dining experiences in the area with a spectacular view of the Gulf of Mexico that just seems to make everything taste a little bit better.

Louisiana Lagniappe (775 Gulf Shore Dr., Holiday Isle, Destin, 850/837-0881, www.thelouisianalagniappe.com, 11am-9:30pm daily Mar.-Oct., no reservations, $15-26) overlooks Old Pass Lagoon and is a local favorite serving upscale Louisiana-style seafood, like pannéed fillet of grouper topped with lobster medallions, lightly covered with garlic beurre blanc. It traffics in live Maine lobsters and has a beautiful outdoor deck.

Marina Cafe (404 Harbor Blvd., Destin, 850/837-7960, www.marinacafe.com, 5pm-10pm daily, $17-28) is another special-occasion destination, moved just slightly in 2007. It's owned by Harbor Restaurant Group, which also owns Destin Chops (a good steak and chop house not far away), with a second Chops location in Seacrest Beach. There's an outdoor dining deck overlooking the Destin Harbor, but inside seating is just as nice. The menu is all over the map, with Cajun/Creole dishes, a sushi bar, and Latin-inspired dishes like grilled Gulf fish tacos with tomato-cucumber salsa, and pan-seared grouper stuffed with lump crab meat and served with a side of Creole succotash.

Beaches of South Walton

The Beaches of South Walton are fairly new. Obviously, the long expanses of white-sand beach have been here all along, but it's in the past 25 years that developers have set their sights on this area. Residents have kept a tight handle on growth—not out of a fear of change as much as a clear vision of how they'd like these communities to meld and enhance their natural settings. Some of it you may find contrived, like Disney for adults, but the idea of New Urbanism has really taken hold with the creation and restoration of compact, walkable, mixed-use towns. Visitors have most of what they need within walking distance of where they're staying, and the Gulf of Mexico and Choctawhatchee Bay are soothing backdrops for a very restful vacation.

Some of these 15 communities actually developed organically, while others were masterminded by architects and savvy developers. From west to east:

Seascape is the closest to Destin, with lakefront and golf villas in an upscale setting. **Miramar Beach** begins at the Gulf along Scenic Gulf Drive and then curves around to join Emerald Coast Parkway. It's mostly condos and private homes and is very close to the Silver Sands Factory Stores. Next up is **Sandestin**, probably the most famous of these little communities, nearly overrun with enormous luxury golf/beach resorts, but all very tasteful. The **Village of Baytowne Wharf** is here in the style of a wealthy but rustic Southern fishing village.

Dune Allen Beach is a quaint and quiet beach community two miles long with mostly classic wood-sided beach houses, homes on a lake, and smaller-sized condo developments. This is where the area's eight-foot-wide,

© JOSHUA LAWRENCE KINSER

THE EMERALD COAST

The Village of Baytowne Wharf's townhomes are within walking distance of restaurants, entertainment, bars, and sugar-white beaches.

RECREATION AT EGLIN AIR FORCE BASE

Eglin Air Force Reservation in Fort Walton Beach is the largest air force base in the free world. It's the size of Rhode Island, covering 724 square miles of reservation and 97,963 square miles of water in the Gulf of Mexico. Eglin employs approximately 10,000 each of military personnel and civilians.

Unless you're in the military, much of it is off limits to you. For instance, Eglin has **two 18-hole championship golf courses** (850/678-8726) open year-round. The Eglin Golf Course, host of a 2000 U.S. Open qualifier, has a hill on the seventh hole so steep that the course provides a towrope to golfers. Here's an interesting tidbit: Al Capone funded the layout of this course originally. In fact, Capone's private beach hideout house is now the officers' club at Eglin.

Much of Eglin you wouldn't want to have access to if you could: The Mother of All Bombs (MOAB), the most powerful nonnuclear bomb ever created, was tested at Eglin. And for years Eglin Air Force Base has been testing depleted uranium (DU), with an estimated 220,000 pounds of DU penetrators expended there since 1973.

The **Air Force Armament Museum** (850/651-1808, 9:30am-4:30pm Mon.-Sat., free admission) is definitely a wonderful public part of Eglin, but it is just one of many opportunities for the visitor. The reservation covers 464,000 acres in Santa Rosa, Okaloosa, and Walton Counties. If you go to the **Jackson Guard** office (107 Hwy. 85 N., Niceville, 850/882-4164) you can get an outdoor recreation permit, a comprehensive map, and a list of regulations. This allows you to explore the area's many activities—hunting, fishing, primitive camping, canoeing, and hiking part of the **Florida National Scenic Trail** (www.floridatrail.org).

Hunting (which accounts for 4,200 of the 12,000 recreation permits granted annually) is for deer, turkey, wild hogs, and small game, seasonally. There's a huge managed quail area, another for "planted" doves, and two duck management units totaling 78,000 acres. There's even an annual hunt open to the mobility-impaired. Fishing in the reservation is on any of 17 stocked ponds (2 of them fully accessible).

Birders will enjoy the old-growth longleaf pine swath of Eglin reservation that is a designated part of the **Great Florida Birding Trail** (www.floridabirdingtrail.com). You may see the endangered Okaloosa darter, found in only six creek systems in the central portion of the air force base. It's also got the fourth-largest red-cockaded woodpecker population in the country. The area is home to more than 90 rare or listed plant and animal species.

Within the reservation there are seven miles of barrier island for swimming and canoeing, with lots of other creeks; enjoy open-water **kayaking** in the Choctawhatchee Bay, Santa Rosa Sound, or the Gulf.

The **Anderson Pond Recreation Area** (off Hwy. 85, 3 miles north of Niceville) is open to the public year-round, with an elevated boardwalk, a picnic shelter, a pier, and a camping area. All the facilities are fully accessible.

off-road bike path begins, winding all the way to Inlet Beach. Fairly developed, **Santa Rosa Beach** has a number of shops and commercial bits, with some golf and beachside amenities. There's a stylish outdoor mall here with boutiques, bike rentals, medical offices, antiques stores, a market, and a big handful of restaurants. Then there's **Blue Mountain Beach,** the highest point along the Gulf of Mexico; with wonderful views and beautiful sand, it has become attractive as an artists' retreat.

Grayton Beach is the oldest town between Pensacola and Apalachicola. Settled in the early 1900s, it is a tree-lined beach community of old cypress cottages and small narrow streets. There is a great bar called the Red Bar that you shouldn't miss, as well as many fine restaurants.

With Seaside to the east fully built out, builders turned not long ago to neighboring **WaterColor,** which is primarily a residential community. Many of the new stylized Cracker-style buildings are available for rent, and the town has a sleek hotel, the 60-room WaterColor Inn.

The next town over is **Seaside,** an upscale, planned beach community of pastel homes and cottages organized around a town square with an outdoor amphitheater, galleries, restaurants, and boutiques. You either love it, using words like "charming" and "picturesque," or you hate it and grumble words like "contrived" and "looks like a stage set" (which it technically was, as the shooting location for *The Truman Show*).

Seagrove Beach is next door to the newer and more fancy Seaside. This peaceful beach town is tucked between the coast's natural sand dunes and pine trees. Visitors can choose from rambling beach houses, cottages, or condos. The very newest community, **WaterSound** is one of the fanciest, with a resort that is plopped right against a pristine coastal dune lake. Then there's **Seacrest Beach,** a newish beach community made up of cottages and condominiums hidden behind natural dunes.

One of my more favorite communities is **Rosemary Beach.** Like Seaside, it's completely planned in a very narrow architectural style, but this time it's all Caribbean-inspired homes connected to the shore by boardwalks and footpaths, with a town square and an exceptional eternity pool.

And finally, **Inlet Beach** is just west of Panama City Beach (over the bridge) and next to Rosemary Beach. Named for the large lagoon on its eastern shore, Phillips Inlet, the peaceful community is known for its secluded natural areas and minimal development.

SIGHTS
C Seaside

It used to be that Americans retreated during the summers to simple beachside cottages for months at a time. Every day, after you got your sunburned hide up off the porch, you biked or walked into the little town center to take in a movie or get the local gossip and an ice cream. In 1946, J. S. Smolian bought 80 acres near Seagrove Beach on Florida's Panhandle with this vision floating in his mind—a utopian

Seaside, where *The Truman Show* was filmed

summer camp for his employees. His grandson, Robert Davis, was smitten by the same vision, growing up to become a fancy developer in Miami in the 1970s. Still, the sweet, multigenerational, seaside summer village eluded him. He infected Miami architects Andres Duany and Elizabeth Plater-Zyberk with his gentle dream, and they built in their minds a fantasy town based on the northwest Florida architectural style of wood-frame cottages with peaked roofs, deep overhangs, and big windows for cross-ventilation. They traveled through Florida with sketchpads and eyes wide open.

Then they made it real in the early 1980s. They built a small town nestled against an idyllic curve along the Gulf Coast shoreline, against a wide swath of beach and mild emerald waters. There are 200 or so homes now, in a paradigm called New Urbanism, situated around a town square with an amphitheater, restaurants, elegant boutiques, a repertory theater, and the beach off at the edge of it all. There's also a much-lauded charter school, a chapel, and a medical arts building. It's a living laboratory—an experiment in harmonious beachside community life.

The kicker is that you can go to Seaside and visit. If you vacation here, you pull your car in, turn off the ignition, and that's the last you need of it for the duration. Everything is within walking distance in what *Time* magazine called "the most astounding design achievement of its era." Panama City is 40 miles to the east, Destin is 20 miles to the west—but Seaside seems miles and miles from anywhere.

SPORTS AND RECREATION

Beaches

Of the numerous beaches along the stretch, many have public beach access, with additional beach accesses located within the 14 beach communities if you're staying there. From west to east, most with access right along scenic Highway 30A, the beaches are Miramar Beach, Legion Park, Cessna Park (on the Choctawhatchee Bay side), Dune Allen Beach, Ed Walline, Gulfview Heights, Blue Mountain Beach, Grayton Dunes, Van Ness Butler Jr.,

Santa Clara, Inlet Beach, and Pier and Boat Ramp 331 (bay side). Which is the nicest is hard to say; most are sparsely populated, many have small, no-fee parking lots, and several have restrooms and showers. My favorite is probably **Santa Clara,** with a beautiful stretch of sand and picnic facilities, but the pristine windswept dunes of **Grayton Dunes** make a very nice afternoon of exploration, too.

Parks and Recreation Areas

There's a large variety of outdoor activities, so bring your most comfortable hiking shoes. At the top of the list is **Grayton Beach State Park** (357 Main Park Rd., south of U.S. 98 halfway between Panama City Beach, near the intersection of Hwy. 30A and County Road 283, 850/267-8300, 8am-sundown daily, $5/vehicle, $2 pedestrian or bicyclist, $24-30 camping, cabin rental $110/day or $705/week), with sugar-white sand, emerald-green water, little development, and huge sea oat-covered sand dunes. Foot traffic is prohibited in the dunes and in bird-nesting areas. Despite its natural setting, there are great restaurants and accommodations in nearby Grayton Beach or Seaside. Camping is popular, with 37 campsites and 30 cabins. Make reservations early. Due to the number of endangered plants and animals found within the park (like the rare Choctawhatchee beach mouse), pets must be kept on a six-foot leash. If you visit in the fall, you may catch the thousands of monarch butterflies resting beachside during their southward migration to Mexico.

Identified as the most pristine piece of coastal property in the state, **Topsail Hill Preserve State Park** (7525 W. Hwy. 30A, in Santa Rosa Beach 10 miles east of Destin, 850/267-8330, 8am-sundown daily, honor $6/vehicle, $2 pedestrian or bicyclist, $42/night for RV camping, $24 tent camping, $100/night and $690/week for bungalows, $130/night for cabins) owes its existence to turpentine. More than a century ago, workers turpentined old-growth longleaf pine trees here for caulking the seams of wooden ships, a key mode of transport. Today, it features 1,600 acres of stunning

COASTAL DUNE LAKES

Think about it for a second: When was the last time you saw a freshwater lake right up against a huge body of saltwater, just a little picturesque sea oat-fringed sand dune separating the two? It appears so gloriously natural that it's easy to overlook, but the Emerald Coast's coastal dune lakes are rare enough to be considered globally imperiled by the Florida Natural Areas Inventory. The 15 in Walton County have sister lakes in a few other spots along the Gulf Coast, then in New Zealand, Australia, and Madagascar. That's it.

These lakes were formed between 2,000 and 10,000 years ago. Coastal winds and flowing tides have kept these water havens safe, separated from the Gulf by ever-changing dune systems ranging 10-30 feet high. Intermittently, when they are swollen with rainwater, the lakes have little wandering fingers that empty out into the Gulf, meaning a canoe or kayak can paddle from freshwater to saltwater and back again without overland toting. These dune lake areas are also biologically diverse with fresh, estuarine, and marine all coexisting in this constant state of flux. Migrating birds are drawn to these coastal lakes as well.

Topsail Hill Preserve State Park has the densest concentration, with Morris, Campbell, and Stalworth Lakes as well as two minor unnamed coastal dune lakes on its property. For more information on the lakes at Topsail Hill Preserve State Park, contact Park Services specialist Leda C. Suydan at 850/267-0299 or Leda.Suydan@dep.state.fl.us.

THE EMERALD COAST

Gulf-front pine forest, nature trails over mountainous sand dunes, and two freshwater dune lakes. It is one of only two remaining natural populations of the nocturnal, endangered Choctawhatchee beach mice. The park features a 140-acre RV resort as well as tent camping and nice bungalows to rent.

In the southernmost portion of Walton County, the 15,000-acre **Point Washington State Forest** (5865 E. U.S. 98, Santa Rosa Beach, 850/267-8325, 8am-sundown daily, $2/person, $20 reserved picnic space) is home to more than 19 miles of trails and boasts 10 different habitats with rare plant and wildlife species, from gopher tortoises to red-cockaded woodpeckers. For an easy day hike, try the Eastern Lake Trail System, the first trail established in this forest. It consists of three double-track loop trails. The hiker or bicyclist can travel the 3.5-, 5-, or 10-mile loops. Access to the trail system is at the parking lot and trailhead on County Road 395.

Nearby, and worth a stop to see, **Eden Gardens State Park** (181 Eden Gardens Rd., off U.S. 98 on County Road 395, just north of Seagrove Beach, 850/267-8320, 8am-sundown daily, honor $4/vehicle, guided tour $4 adults, $2 children), in historic Point Washington on the shore of Tucker Bayou, is a beautiful 1895 Greek Revival estate surrounded by gardens of azaleas, camellias, and large moss-draped live oak. This 12-acre sprawling park was once the home of lumber baron William Henry Wesley and his family. Find yourself a picnic spot on the wide, manicured lawn.

Just east of Seagrove Beach, **Deer Lake State Park** (357 Main Park Rd., off Hwy. 30A, Santa Rosa Beach, 850/267-8300, 8am-sundown daily, $3/vehicle, $2 pedestrian or bicyclist) is the newest park in these parts. It has an excellent beach with a dune walkover/boardwalk, from which there are great views of this dynamic dune ecosystem. North of here are acres of hiking trails worth exploring.

If you're interested in enjoying all this nature within the context of an ecotour or guided adventure, there are plenty of guides in the area. **Blue Sky Kayak Tours** (89 Lakeside Dr., Freeport, 850/368-3155) offers guided tours in different local habitats. **Choctawhatchee Delta Tours** (710 Black Creek Rd., Freeport, 850/585-0445) also offers tours of this area, departing from the 331 Bridge. **Baytowne Watersports** (801 Kell-Aire Dr., Destin,

850/699-2511), formerly Island Winds Sailing, has catamarans for sailing, offering ecotours, lessons, sunset/moonlight cruises, and sand dollar excursions. And **Big Daddy's Bike and Beach** (2217 Hwy. 30A, Santa Rosa Beach, 850/622-1165) offers bike rentals and ecotours on bike along Highway 30A and through a state forest area.

Seaside Swim & Tennis Club (corner of Forest and Odessa Sts., 850/231-2214, 8am-4pm Mon.-Sat., 8am-2pm Sun.) is at the center of lots of the town's activities. It offers private tennis lessons and clinics for kids and adults, shuffleboard and horseshoes, bike rentals (including trikes), and three beautiful croquet courts. There are three pools—the West Side Pool is the largest, with an adult pool at the north end of Seaside Avenue and a family pool at the northeast corner of Seaside. **Camp Seaside** is a special program for kids 5-12, with half-day or full-day crafts, sports, swimming, and other activities. It also offers a kids' night out, with dinner and a movie, and regularly scheduled free storytime in the amphitheater.

Beyond that, Seaside has nearby golf, a long biking/walking path, deep-sea fishing, hiking, kayaking, and swimming in the Gulf to keep everyone occupied.

◖ Biking Along Scenic Route 30A

The **Timpoochee Trail** is one of the longest and most widely used paths in Walton County. The 19-mile, paved trail winds through 9 of the 14 distinctive beach communities, traversing state recreational areas, state parks, dunes, and coastal dune lakes. Named after Timpoochee Kinnard, the most influential Indian chief of the Euchee Indians, the path runs along Scenic Highway 30A parallel to the Gulf of Mexico. From migrating flocks of birds to blooming wildflowers and trees, the Timpoochee Trail is full of surprises all year long. Hop off the bike for an ice cream. Rent a bike with a basket and pick up some groceries for dinner along the way—a paperback from Sundog Books, maybe a bottle of wine for the sunset.

This is road or touring bike territory. For the mountain biker, there is also a 10-mile loop in the Point Washington State Forest called the **Eastern Lake Bike/Hike Trail,** which winds through natural vegetation and wildlife habitat. A new stretch of trail goes to Seagrove, or go in the opposite direction for a scenic ride from Seaside to Blue Mountain Beach.

And then there's the **Longleaf Pine Greenway System** (850/231-5800), interlaced through several state parks and forests, with eight miles of trails through different terrain from the Gulf to Choctawhatchee Bay. Most bike shops will equip you with maps of the different cycling possibilities in the area.

Depending on where you're staying, there are several convenient bike rental shops. From west to east: **Seaside Bike Shop** (87 Central Square, Seaside, 850/231-2314, $30/day, $65/5 days), **Butterfly Bike & Beach Rentals** (3657 E. Hwy. 30A, Seagrove Beach, 850/231-2826, with Caloi off-road bikes), and **Bamboo Beach & Bicycle Company** (50 N. Barrett Square, Rosemary Beach, 850/231-0770, $20/day, $45/3 days, $70/week, children's bikes $16/day, $40/3 days, $65/week).

Fishing

Baytowne Marina at Sandestin is a good place to start. **Baytowne Bait and Tackle Store** (Sandestin, 850/267-7777) provides basic boating necessities, and it's a good place to hook up with a fishing guide. Similarly, **Old Florida Outfitters** (WaterColor, 850/534-4343), an Orvis-endorsed guide program, is a great source for specialized fishing charters, located in WaterColor's Town Center.

Not A Dog Charters (850/267-2514, www.notadogcharters.com) heads out from Grayton Beach; after a short boat ride you'll be bottom fishing for red snapper, grouper, and trigger fish, or trolling for king mackerel. In the spring, the target is cobia right along the beach. **Yellow Fin Ocean Sports** (850/231-9024) in Grayton will take you fishing for redfish or trout in coastal bays or head out into the Gulf for grouper, snapper, dolphin, or marlin. **Dead Fish Charters** (174 WaterColor Way #280, Seagrove Beach, 850/685-1092, www.deadfish-charters.com) specializes in Indian Pass half- or full-day trips, and inshore grouper and snapper trips in Grayton Beach.

SHOPPING

Shopping is clustered in a handful of tasteful centers along the Beaches of South Walton. The **Market Shops at Sandestin** (9375 U.S. 98 W. at Sandestin Golf & Beach Resort, 850/650-3164) complex has 30 shops, split between kitchenware, skin care, chocolates, housewares, and more. The **Shops of Grayton** (26 Logan Ln., Grayton Beach) are not as upscale, and here you'll find jewelry, clothing, and antiques. In Seaside there is **Ruskin Place Artist Colony** near the new Seaside Chapel and the rest of the 40 or so **Merchants of Seaside** (63 Central Square, 850/231-5424) for cafés, galleries, clothing, books, and gifts. Head to the Beaches of South Walton, especially Seaside, if you're looking for art. This area is increasingly a hotbed of independent art galleries.

Ruskin Place, named after John Ruskin, the famous supporter of 19th-century art, is the town's center for galleries, with a good coffee shop and a few other diversions. There are plenty of shops worth a bit of exploration in Seaside, but definitely check out the vessels, chandeliers, sinks, and other blown-glass art of **Fusion Art Glass** (55 Central Square, 850/231-5405, www.fusionartglass.com). **Sundog Books** (89 Central Square, 850/231-5481) is a great place in the area to spend a few hours. The current fiction is always in stock, along with plenty of art and design books.

ACCOMMODATIONS
Resorts and Vacation Rentals

The **Hilton Sandestin Beach Golf Resort & Spa** (4000 Sandestin Blvd. S., Destin, 850/267-9500, www.sandestinbeachhilton.com, $149-259) is an extremely beautiful golf-and-spa resort of 598 rooms, the largest beachfront resort hotel in the northwest Florida region. There are 190 spacious standard guest rooms, 22 parlor suites, two presidential suites, and 385 junior suites that feature bunk beds with portholes in the sides for a nautical style and a private gaming system that kids will surely

THE EMERALD COAST

© JOSHUA LAWRENCE KINSER

Sandestin offers a long stretch of accommodations along the coast.

Sandestin Golf & Beach Resort

appreciate. The hotel has an award-winning program for children, with accessible on-site dining at Sandcastles Restaurant & Lounge, which has a great breakfast buffet in the morning. There's also a fancier restaurant called Seagar's Prime Steaks & Seafood that has a long sushi bar lining the back. The wine room located in the front of the restaurant is separated from the rest of the dining room and doubles as an intimate and private dining room. You can reserve the space for a small party or couple and hold your special occasion in a romantic setting surrounded by racks of the wine bottles that make up the restaurant's extensive wine list.

So many of the nicer accommodations around here are private homes or condos. There are numerous property management companies—the **Beach Rental of South Walton** website (www.brswvacations.com) is a good place to start surfing for what you want. It's divided by community, specializing in the more affordable ones. Many of the swankier communities have their own websites with rental information

and slide shows (www.rosemarybeach.com, www.seasidefl.com). My favorite is definitely ⟨ **Rosemary Beach** (on Hwy. 30A, in between Seacrest and Inlet Beach, 850/278-2030, www.rosemarybeach.com, roughly $200-500/night, but many rentals are by the week), with one- to five-bedroom Gulf-front and midtown cottages for vacation rentals. All designed in a loose Caribbean style, there are family cottages, carriage houses, flats, and contemporary lofts, all connected to the shore by boardwalks and footpaths. It's a good location for families, because it's farther east than many of the communities, and thus closer to the liveliness of Panama City Beach but still out of the fray.

Then there's the **Sandestin Golf & Beach Resort** (9300 Emerald Coast Pkwy. W., Sandestin, 850/267-8000, $172-450), really the premier resort in this area, set on 2,400 beach- and bay-front acres. There are four championship golf courses, 15 world-class tennis courts, a full-service marina, water sports, charter sailing and fishing, fine and casual dining, a fancy fitness center, a professional salon and day spa, and fun children's programs. If you want to improve your game, professional golf and tennis trainers on-site use the most advanced swing analysis technology available. It's got 1,350 different rooms and accommodations, with a range of options—it's kind of like a little city unto itself, with leisure as the town's central preoccupation.

Really, the city in question is **Village of Baytowne Wharf** (9300 Emerald Coast Pkwy. W., Sandestin, 850/267-8000, $180-800), a sweeping pedestrian village right on the beach that rents its own accommodations. There are different choices on where to stay, grouped into five resort areas: Beachfront, Beachside, Village, Bayside, and Dockside. Each of the five Florida resorts offers a unique flavor, as well as a range of rates. Included with a stay at any of the resort accommodations options are free kayak, canoe, and bike rentals. The resort is also the host of many area festivals including the Sandestin Wine Festival and, my favorite, the Baytowne Beer Festival. They are also starting to host outdoor concerts with large nationally recognized acts. When I was there Vince Gill was performing on the grounds of the resort, so make sure to check the events calendar on the extensive website to see what's on the agenda.

To **rent a cottage at Seaside,** you need only to call 888/541-0801. The tricky part comes in figuring out what you want—people have built their dream homes in Seaside, and the prices, styles, and sizes are all over the map. There are more than 200 homes and cottages. It offers 400 individual accommodations, including private homes, cottages, luxury townhouses, penthouses, and beachfront hideaways.

Camping

The only way to slide in under $50 around here is by camping—it's warm much of the year, with nice evening breezes, lots of beach, plenty of fresh air, and not so rural that you can't go out for dinner. One of the best places in the area to camp is located in the town of Grayton Beach near Seaside at **Grayton Beach State Park** (357 Main Park Rd., south of U.S. 98 halfway between Panama City Beach and Destin, near the intersection of Hwy. 30A and County Road 283, 850/267-8300, 8am-sundown daily, $5/vehicle, $2/pedestrian or bicyclist, $24-30 camping, cabin rental $110/day or $705/week). The campground has 34 sites accommodating tents and RVs and is located right on the Gulf of Mexico among trees and dunes. It has restrooms, electricity, and hot showers to rinse away those hours of swimming and wading in the salty warm waters of the Gulf of Mexico before you roast some marshmallows over an open fire with the waves of the Gulf lapping in the background.

In Sandestin you can camp on the Gulf at **CampGulf RV Park and Campground** (10005 W. Emerald Coast Pkwy., Destin, 850/226-7485, campsites $55-180, cabins $100-300), with an activity center, fishing, cable TV, and full hookups. **Destin RV Beach Resort** (362 Miramar Beach Dr., Destin, 850/837-3529) is hands-down the nicest RV campground I have come across. The owners call it a "luxury RV resort." It is right across from the beach, with a

swimming pool and a free deep-sea fishing trip with a paid stay.

You can also camp at **Topsail Hill Preserve State Park** (7525 W. Hwy. 30A, in Santa Rosa Beach 10 miles east of Destin, 850/267-8330, 8am-sundown daily, $6/vehicle, $2 pedestrian or bicyclist, $42/night RVs and $24 tents, $100/night and $690/week for bungalows, $130/night and $850/week for cabins) at the Topsail Hill Gregory E. Moore RV Resort, which has the highest possible rating from *Trailer Life* and Woodall's, placing it in the top 1 percent of RV campgrounds in the nation. The campground has a stunning 156 RV sites with electricity, sewer, water, and cable. It also offers 22 tent sites with electricity. The park has a swimming pool, bathrooms, hot showers, and a camp store with water, other drinks, snacks, and camping items. A tram will give you a lift to the beach. It's definitely more set up for RV enthusiasts, but it's a good place to tent camp as well if there aren't any sites left at Grayton Beach State Park.

FOOD

All of the little communities of South Walton have their own cluster of restaurants, in a range of price points and culinary traditions. A few I would recommend include **◖ Bud and Alley's Restaurant** (2236 E. Hwy. 30A, Seaside, 850/231-5900, lunch 11:30am-3pm daily, dinner 5:30pm-9pm Sun.-Thurs., 5:30pm-9:30pm Fri.-Sat., rooftop bar 11:30am-2am daily, $20-28), which opened in Seaside in 1986 and is actually named after a dog and a cat. It's an upscale yet casual and unpretentious place, with a cooking style that nods to the coastal Mediterranean, Basque country, Tuscany, and the American Deep South. Oysters Seaside are baked Apalachicola beauties with shrimp, scallops, calamari, cilantro, garlic, and lime, and there are tempura-fried soft-shell crabs with rémoulade, or heads-on shrimp with garlic and shallots. The bar has an extensive wine list and is a great spot for conversation with the locals.

Chef Jim Shirley brings his brand of Southern cooking to Seaside at the **Great Southern Café** (83 Central Square, Seaside, 850/231-7327,

8am-9:30pm daily, $10-28). The menu's regional flair includes Gulf shrimp, Apalachicola oysters, and traditional Southern vegetables. It seems like no one talks about the Great Southern Café without mentioning the Grits a Ya Ya, one of the most-ordered dishes, which offers seasoned shrimp in smoked gouda cheese grits topped with cream gravy, bacon, spinach, and mushrooms. **Dawson's Yogurt** (121 Central Square, Seaside, 850/231-4770, 10am-9pm Sun.-Thurs., 10am-10pm Fri.-Sat.) is the place to indulge in your choice of over 20 flavors of yogurt. The Kahlua fudge is a favorite.

Cafe Thirty-A (3899 E. Hwy. 30A, Seagrove, 850/231-2166, 5pm-10pm daily, $12-34) is another upscale spot, with a large wine list, many selections by the glass. The menu has broad appeal, with dishes such as wood oven-roasted grouper served with baby tiger shrimp and risotto in a sweet carrot sauce or maple barbecue pork chop with fried peaches and corn mashed potatoes on the side. I'm pretty content just to slice up one of the Hawaiian-style wood-fired pizzas.

Next there's **Basmati's Asian Cuisine** (3295 W. Hwy. 30A, Blue Mountain Beach, 850/267-3028, lunch 11am-3pm Mon.-Fri., dinner 5pm-10pm daily, $9-28) with a full sushi bar and mostly Japanese fusion dishes served in a beautiful dining room and a nice sheltered deck.

In the Village of Baytowne Wharf, you've got **Graffiti's & The Funky Blues Shack** (109 Cannery Ln., Sandestin, 850/424-6650, 5pm-10pm daily, $12-23), a folk art-infused restaurant and live blues venue, or **New Orleans Creole Cookery** (Village of Baytowne Wharf, Sandestin, 850/351-1885, 11am-9pm Sun.-Thurs., 11am-10pm Fri.-Sat., $15-30)—if you've got the Nola jones, head here, especially for the barbecued shrimp and Creole bread pudding.

For breakfast, top honors go to Rosemary Beach's **Wild Olives Market** (104 N. Barrett Square, Rosemary Beach, 850/231-0065, 10am-8pm Tues.-Sat., 10am-6pm Sun.) or **Summer Kitchen** (60 N. Barrett Square, Rosemary Beach, 850/231-6264, 7:30am-9pm daily) for pastries and egg dishes; for a glass of wine, stop off at nearby **Courtyard Wine and Cheese** (66 Main St. in the Gourd Garden Courtyard, Rosemary Beach, 850/231-1219, 2pm-10pm Tues.-Sun.), with 50 wines by the glass.

Locals have been flocking to **Wine World** (WaterColor Town Center, 850/231-1323, 10am-5pm daily), a low-key neighborhood wine, beer, and cheese shop that also serves a fine selection of coffees, pizzas, paninis, and tapas. It's right in WaterColor Market in the heart of Town Center, an easy place to hang out and enjoy the effects of a relaxing beach vacation.

Panama City Beach

Panama City Beach gets billed as the No. 1 spring break beach in the country, attracting more than 300,000 people annually. The hottest spring break places change, though. In the 1980s it was places like Palm Springs or Fort Lauderdale; for a while after that people seemed more focused on Cancún, Mazatlán, or Cabo San Lucas. Most recently Puerto Vallarta and Miami Beach are neck and neck for spring break mania.

Yet Panama City Beach attracts a huge crowd of young people ready to throw down for spring break and has a ton of attractions to keep them entertained. The city even publishes a booklet for spring breakers that outlines the attractions in the area they are most likely to enjoy. With the same green water and white-sand found elsewhere on the Emerald Coast, these beaches are more action-oriented, with volleyball, Frisbee, skim boarding, Jet Skiing, and parasailing. Although the beach is wide with a lengthy expanse of shallows, there are hundreds of natural and artificial reefs offshore—Panama City Beach ranks with Key Largo in providing some of the best diving in the country. The fishing is also good, with

Panama City Beach

mackerel, flounder, redfish, and other game fish swimming through the clear waters.

At the east end of the city, St. Andrews State Park is fabulous, one of the most popular outdoor recreation spots in Florida. It contains verdant woods, sea oat-fringed sand dunes, fresh- and saltwater marshes, a lagoon swimming area, fishing jetties, hiking trails, 2.5 miles of beach, and two campgrounds. From here, you can also take a pedestrian ferry to Shell Island, an undisturbed 700-acre barrier island just across from the mainland, for sunning, shelling, birding, or watching the sunset.

Outside of the beaches, the area is known for its roadside attractions like miniature golf, waterslide parks, go-cart tracks, and a marine park. The Miracle Strip, which lent Panama City Beach its name as a nickname, was a beloved amusement park—one of the area's biggest draws—but it closed in 2004.

So, we know it's packed in March and April, and tourists from Georgia and Alabama flock to PCB during the summer. But in the early fall or during May, between the hordes, Panama City Beach makes for an entertaining beachside playground, with loads of modestly priced accommodations. It's at these times that you can understand why the area has been a popular beach vacation spot for more than 40 years.

SPORTS AND RECREATION
Diving and Snorkeling

Panama City Beach was dubbed the Shipwreck Capital of the South by *Skin Diver* magazine. As such, this part of the warm Gulf of Mexico is an excellent home and breeding ground for all types of sea life. You'll see sea turtles, manta rays, puffer fish, sand dollars, blue marlin, horseshoe crabs, small coral, colorful sponges, and lots of other marine life.

Of the "natural" wrecks in this area, you can investigate a 441-foot **World War II Liberty ship,** a 220-foot tug called **The Chippewa,** a 160-foot coastal freighter called the **S.S. Tarpon,** the 100-foot tug **Chickasaw,** another tug called **The Grey Ghost,** and the Gulf's most famous wreck, the 465-foot **Empire Mica.** A bunch of other artificial reef projects have sunk bridge spans, barges, and the City of Atlantis (a different one). Many of these dive sites are at depths of 80-100 feet and are just a few miles offshore; the best time for diving is April-September.

Experts say that the top five dives are the **USS Strength,** a naval mine sweeper; the **Blackbart,** a supply vessel; another supply vessel called the **B. J. Putnam;** the **Accokeek,** a 295-foot navy tug boat; and a huge aluminum **hovercraft** in 100 feet of water. If you want to rent diving equipment, **Dive Locker** (106 Thomas Dr., 850/230-8006), **Diver's Den** (6222 E. Business Hwy., 850/871-6889), **Panama City Dive Center** (4823 Thomas Dr., 850/235-3390), and the **Dixie Divers** (109 W. 23rd St., 850/914-9988) will help you out.

Snorkelers will have a better time around the **St. Andrews Jetties,** an area with no boat traffic. Nineteen feet under the surface there is an old tar barge ideal for underwater exploration. If you want to snorkel with a guide, **Island Time** (Treasure Island Marina, 3605 Thomas Dr., 850/234-7377, adults $39, children 3 and under $29) offers 3.5-hour catamaran excursions, wet suits available, and **Captain Ashley Gorman Shell Island Cruises** (5701 U.S. 98, east end of Hathaway Bridge, 850/785-4878, $40/person) does swim and snorkeling tours for the whole family.

⬤ St. Andrews State Park

St. Andrews State Park (4607 State Park Ln., Panama City, 850/233-5140, 8am-sundown daily, $4/single driver, $8/vehicle 2-8 people, $2 pedestrians or bicyclists, $28 camping) has rolling, white-sand dunes separated by low swales of either pinewoods or marshes. There are 2.5 miles of beach, with two different parking lots with access. You can rent bicycles during the summer at the park and explore the trails. There's a double-sided concrete boat launch for watercraft (if don't own a boat, you can take a boat tour out to Shell Island in the spring and summer, tickets at the park concession), and they rent canoes at the boat ramp (paddle around Grand Lagoon or across the boat channel to Shell Island). If you want to

fish, there are two fishing piers and jetties, from which you're likely to catch Spanish mackerel, redfish, flounder, sea trout, bonito, cobia, dolphin, and bluefish. The concession stores in the park sell bait and fishing licenses, along with other beachside necessities. For hikers, there's Heron Pond Trail (starting at a reconstructed Cracker turpentine still) and Gator Lake Trail (yep, you'll see gators), both easy and well marked. And if it's all too great to leave, there are 176 campsites in the park or on the barrier Shell Island.

Other Recreation Areas

All the other parks around here get overshadowed by St. Andrews, which is a shame. **Pine Log State Forest** (5583-A Longleaf Rd., Ebro, 850/535-2888) is a favorite locals' spot for picnicking, hiking, off-road bicycling, horseback riding, fishing, and hunting. There are 23 miles of hiking trails winding through the forest. Nearby **Point Washington State Forest** (5865 U.S. 98 E., Santa Rosa Beach, 850/267-8325) is less developed but has 19 miles of trails for mountain biking, birding, and hunting.

In general, the whole area has benefited from the completion of a U.S Army Corp of Engineers beach re-nourishment project, Florida's longest continuous beach restoration. The $23.5 million project elevated and widened a 16.5-mile stretch of beach by an average of 30 feet, with something like a billion cubic yards of new, white sand. Besides beautifying the shoreline, the re-nourishment provides critical storm protection.

SIGHTS

The biggest local thrills around here used to be at the Miracle Strip Amusement Park, which closed in 2004. Let us observe a moment of silence.

Now the best family attraction is to be had at **Gulf World** (15412 Front Beach Rd., 850/234-5271, 9am-7pm daily March-Aug., 9:30am-5pm daily Sept.-Feb., $28 adults, $18 children 5-11, children 4 and under free), which got pumped up seriously around the millennium, with a $6.5 million expansion that netted it a state-of-the-art dolphin habitat, a new bird theater, and enclosed tropical gardens. It needed it. The marine mammal park opened in 1969 with animal shows and displays, but it also has a facility to rehabilitate stranded or injured marine animals from all over the Panhandle. As with so many of Florida's aquariums and water parks, there is a swim-with-the-dolphins option to the tune of $175 per person (also a trainer for a day program and a slumber-party option).

Coconut Creek Family Fun Park (9807 Front Beach Rd., 850/234-2625, www.coconutcreekfun.com, 10am-6pm daily, $18 one price, $10.50 just for golf, $9.50 just for gran maze—why there's no "d" on that is a mystery) has two miniature golf courses in a kind of African safari/jungle motif. The maze is the better part, built in 1987 and completely rebuilt recently. It's a huge, human-sized maze the size of a football field in which you will find disoriented children and lots of military personnel using their professional navigational skills to find the four checkpoints (for some reason, they are Fiji, Tahiti, Samoa, and Bali) essential to successfully navigating the maze. There's no shame in crawling under to get the heck out of here. Well, maybe a little shame.

Shipwreck Island Water Park (12201 Middle Beach Rd., 850/234-3333, www.shipwreckisland.com, 10:30am-5:30pm daily summer, $33 50 inches and above, $28 35-49 inches, under 35 inches free, $22 seniors) is the kind of water park with long slides and flumes, a wave pool, kiddie pools—in other words, what to do if the beach isn't holding the kids' interest for another warm summer day. There is a 48-inch height restriction on two of the more exciting rides (the Rapid River Run and Tree Top Drop), and you're not allowed to bring food in from outside, or flotation devices, goggles, or masks. Little ones not yet potty-trained are required to wear waterproof swim diapers.

Need more to do? There's a **Ripley's Believe It or Not! Museum** (9907 Front Beach Rd., 850/230-6113, 10am-10pm daily, $15.99 adults, $10.99 children 6-12) with all the requisite shrunken heads and scale models of the Lusitania made out of ear wax. OK, I made

that one up. Nearby you'll find **Zoo World Zoological and Botanical Park** (9008 Front Beach Rd., 850/230-1243, 9:30am-4pm Mon.-Sat., 11am-4pm Sun., $16 adults, $10 children 4-11, $12 seniors 65 and over), a small and pleasant zoo. The best part is the interspecies interaction between Tonda the orangutan and T. K. the tabby cat. Little kids will really enjoy **Sea Dragon Pirate Cruise** (departs from 5325 N. Lagoon Dr., 850/234-7400, $24 adults, $18 children 14 and under, $20 seniors 60 and older, times vary, reservations highly recommended), a cruise with Captain Phil on a totally kitted out pirate ship, heavy on the "argh." **Museum of Man in the Sea** (17314 Panama City Beach Pkwy., 850/235-4101, 10am-5pm Wed.-Sat., $5, children under 7 free) is a small but very interesting museum that delves into the history of deep sea diving and ocean exploration.

SHOPPING
Pier Park
Shopping, dining, and entertainment are all within easy reach at Pier Park, new in 2008. This 900,000-square-foot retail and entertainment complex sits on 93 acres in the heart of downtown across from the City Pier. Target, Panera Bread, The Grand 16-Plex Theatres, and Longhorn Steakhouse were the first establishments to open. It is anchored by a 125,000-square-foot Dillard's, JCPenney, and Jimmy Buffet's Margaritaville restaurant and nightclub, with smaller stores including Ron Jon Surf Shop, Starbucks, Ann Taylor Loft, Ulta Cosmetics, Victoria's Secret, Bath & Body Works, and more. Its open-air eateries take best advantage of gorgeous Gulf views.

Beyond that, there are little pockets of shops all over, mostly of the sunglasses-and-suntan-lotion variety. You may need to stock up on bathing suits at **Beach Scene Superstore** (10059 Hutchinson Blvd., 850/233-1662), which has something like 25,000 suits to try on. If you feel the need for more extensive browsing, the **Shoppes at Edgewater** (4412 Delwood Ln., 850/234-6112) complex has a number of nice shops. Also, the Edgewater Movie Theater and

Rock-It Lanes Family Entertainment Center are adjacent to the shopping center. **Panama City Mall** (at the intersection of U.S. 231, Hwy. 77, and 23rd St., 850/785-9587) is a standard enclosed mall anchored by Dillard's, JCPenney, and Sears, with stores like American Eagle Outfitters, Victoria's Secret, Kirkland's, Bath & Body Works, The Gap, and Express.

Spas

The spa industry makes up the fourth-largest leisure industry in the United States, something Panama City Beach has jumped on with a vengeance in recent years. The toniest might be the 12,025-square-foot **Serenity at Bay Point** (4114 Jan Cooley Dr., 850/236-6028), but there's also the **Spa at Majestic Beach Resort** (10901 Front Beach Rd., 866/494-3364), and the **Spa at the Edgewater Beach and Golf Resort** (11212 Front Beach Rd., 855/874-8686).

ACCOMMODATIONS

It seems that all of Panama City Beach has been under construction in the past few years, with condos, resorts, hotels, town homes, and villas transforming the destination. Panama City Beach has recently completed over 30 resort and condominium projects, many big high-rises set right against the beach. Inventory has grown to an all-time high of more than 30,000 rooms. Due to the surplus of rooms in the off-season during the fall and winter months, you can find some of the best deals on the Gulf Coast right here in Panama City Beach.

Under $50

The **Sandpiper Beacon** (17403 Front Beach Rd., 850/234-2154, $39-100) is a comfortable, family-friendly place with lots of on-site amenities for the price. It has 1,000 feet of beachfront, with parasailing, personal watercraft, and the Big Banana Ride right out the back door. There are three pools (one indoor), a lazy river ride, and twin turbo waterslides, a game room, restaurant, children's playground, gift shop, and tiki bar. There are family units, with some suites sleeping up to 10 people.

Super 8 Panama City Beach (207 U.S. 231, between Hwy. 77 and U.S. 98, 850/784-1988, $39-80) is another no-frills home base close to the beach. It has clean rooms and very basic amenities, but get this: During March and April a deposit of $200 is required, and you have to wear *wristbands* to prove you're actually staying here and aren't just crashing the joint.

$100-150

Chateau Motel (12525 Front Beach Rd., 888/842-3224, $100-200) is a favorite among young people, with 150 Gulf-view rooms 500 feet from the sand. It's right at the center of all the Miracle Strip excitement, with restaurants, attractions, shopping, and nightlife within walking distance. If you're under 25, they make you pay an extra $100 deposit until you pass checkout inspection.

Days Inn Beach Hotel (12818 Front Beach Rd., 850/233-3333, $115-180) is hopping, with 188 Gulf-front rooms and suites with private balconies. Room decor is tropical and breezy, but you'll spend most of your time outside at the seven-story volcano mountain waterfall. It's in the huge pool situated between the Days Inn and Ramada Limited. It's a scene out there, with athletic young people sipping tropical drinks and flirting shamelessly in the whirlpool.

Over $150

The very upscale **C Grand Panama Beach Resort** (11800 and 11807 Front Beach Rd., 850/316-8964, www.grandpanamabeachresort. com, $149 and up) is a 35-acre resort cuddled against a 240-foot stretch of beach, the property featuring 299 units spread out over two beachfront towers, two pools and spas, a fitness center and two tiki bars, plus a playground, game room, and a jogging/bicycle path around the perimeter of the property. Besides its own on-site concert venue, the resort is also home to the Village of Grand Panama, a 55,000-square-foot retail center with an array of shops, services, and restaurants, including a spa and salon, a wine shop, and several clothing boutiques. Additionally, the property offers guests free high-speed Internet access, including Wi-Fi in designated outdoor and poolside areas. Guests staying at Grand Panama Beach Resort are granted exclusive access to the Sterling Club at Bay Point, featuring northwest Florida's only Nicklaus-designed golf course, the Serenity Spa at Bay Point, tennis, dining, and a water-sports marina.

Edgewater Beach Resort (11212 Front Beach Rd., 850/235-4044, $81-516) is worth the splurge; it's really Panama City Beach's premier resort and very family-friendly. It's a great location on the beach, right across the street from Cinema 10 Theaters, Rock-It Lanes, miniature golf, and the Shoppes at Edgewater. On-site there are two restaurants, two bars, 11 heated outdoor pools, an executive 9-hole golf course, and the 27-hole Hombre Golf Club championship course just minutes away. The rooms themselves are spread throughout a vast property, from the Gulf Front Towers to the Golf and Tennis Villas to the Windward and Leeward Suites.

Another excellent place, a bit removed from the fray, is the **Marriott's Legends Edge at Bay Point** (4000 Marriott Dr., 850/236-4200, $280-419). Each villa has a fully equipped kitchen, spacious living and dining areas, and well-appointed bedrooms. It's adjacent to the Marriott Bay Point Resort Village and situated in the midst of the Club Meadows and Lagoons Legends golf courses (designed by Bob von Hagge and Bruce Devlin in 1985, and a notoriously challenging course). The Gulf of Mexico is 10 minutes away, and the Grand Lagoon of St. Andrews Bay is within walking distance.

FOOD

In Panama City Beach you mostly get fried seafood, wings, pizza, and burgers—the sort of food you would expect from a location mostly supported by college students. Yet there are some great restaurants for all tastes. One option is to keep it simple, heading for familiar offerings like **Bonefish Grill, Carrabba's Italian Grill,** or **Ruth's Chris Steakhouse.** For a great cheeseburger, go to **Flamingo Joe's** (2304 Thomas Dr., 850/233-0600, 11am-9pm daily, $8-15). It also has an addictive salsa, served warm. **Sharky's Beachfront Seafood Restaurant** (15201 Front Beach Rd., 850/235-2420, 11am-10pm daily, $15-27) is a longstanding favorite for a good sunset, fine live entertainment in the world's largest tiki hut, and seafood-centric food.

The Boat Yard (5323 N. Lagoon Dr., 850/249-9273, 11am-11pm daily, later on the weekend if things are hopping, $10-26) has a similar open-air feel on the docks of Grand Lagoon, with gigantic margaritas, conch fritters with hot pepper jelly and wasabi mayo, crispy fried lobster sandwiches, and a really tasty dessert invention of creamy key lime pie dipped in dark chocolate and frozen on a stick. **J' Michaels** (3210 Thomas Dr., 850/233-2055, 11am-9pm daily, $8-15) is dockside of Grand Lagoon and is the place to go for comfort food like red beans and rice.

You want to take it a little more upscale? **Angelo's Steak Pit** (9527 Front Beach Rd., 850/234-2351, 5pm-10pm daily, closed in the winter, $14-26) always gets the nod for fat steaks grilled over aromatic hickory. It's been here since 1958, and the resident 20,000-pound steer, Big Gus, is practically a local celebrity.

Captain Anderson's Restaurant (5550 N. Lagoon Dr., 850/234-2225, 4:30pm-10pm Mon.-Fri., 4pm-10pm Sat., $12-35) is another serious locals' establishment, focusing on seafood. It's a waterfront favorite that's been here for years—go for the heads-on shrimp or the open-hearth whole fish.

Information and Services

The Emerald Coast area is located within the **central time zone.** The area code is **850.**

TOURIST INFORMATION

The Panama City **News Herald** is the daily around here, but its parent company, Halifax Media Group, also operates the **Northwest Florida Daily News,** the **Destin Log,** the **Walton Sun,** and www.emeraldcoast.com.

To get tourist information, there are several different locations, depending on where your home base is. For Destin and Fort Walton Beach information, visit the **Emerald Coast Convention & Visitors Bureau** (1540 E. U.S. 98, Fort Walton Beach, 850/651-7131, www.emeraldcoastfl.com). There's also the **South Walton Tourist Development Center** (25771 U.S. 331 at U.S. 98, Santa Rosa Beach, 850/267-1216, 8am-5pm daily) and the **Destin Area Chamber of Commerce** (4484 Legendary Dr. at U.S. 98, 850/837-6241, 8:30am-5pm Tues.-Fri.).

For information about the Beaches of South Walton area in advance of your trip, contact the **Beaches of South Walton Tourist Development Council** (P.O. Box 1248, Santa Rosa Beach, FL 32459, 800/822-6877, www.visitsouthwalton.com).

In Panama City Beach, visit the **Panama City Beach Convention & Visitors Bureau** (17001 Panama City Beach Pkwy., 850/233-5070, www.visitpanamacitybeach.com, 8am-5pm daily) for brochures, maps, and information about attractions and accommodations.

POLICE AND EMERGENCIES

In an emergency, dial 911. For a nonemergency police need, call or visit the **Fort Walton Beach Police Department** (7 Hollywood Blvd., Fort Walton Beach, 850/833-9546) or the **Panama City Beach Police Department** (17110 Firenzo Ave., Panama City Beach, 850/233-5000).

In the event of a medical emergency, stop into **Sacred Heart Hospital on the Emerald Coast** (7800 U.S. 98 W., Miramar Beach, 850/278-3000) in the western part of the Emerald Coast; in the eastern part, go to **Bay Medical Center** (615 N. Bonita Ave., Panama City, 850/769-1511).

RADIO AND TELEVISION

There's lots of music radio in this area, heavy on rock and pop for all those spring breakers. **Beach 99.9 FM** is oldies, **94.5 FM** is talk radio, **92.5 FM** has country, **Sunny 98.5 FM** is soft rock, and **93.5 FM** is urban.

And on the television, there are two local ABC affiliates, **WMBB Channel 13** out of Panama City and **WEAR Channel 3** out of Pensacola. The CBS affiliate is **WCTV Channel 6** out of Tallahassee, the PBS affiliate is **WFSG Channel 56** out of Panama City, and the NBC affiliate is **WJHG Channel 7** out of Panama City.

LAUNDRY SERVICES

Laundry options are at their best in Panama City Beach. There's **Flamingo Beach Laundry** (7922 Front Beach Rd., 850/234-6186) or **EBR Laundry** (11309 Hutchinson Blvd., 850/235-4077).

Getting There and Around

BY CAR

Ground travel is easy around the Emerald Coast, along several primary feeders: U.S. 98, U.S. 331, Highway 85, and I-10. Fort Walton Beach, the hometown of Eglin Air Force Base, is 60 miles west of Panama City and 35 miles east of Pensacola. U.S. 98 travels east-west along the Emerald Coast, edging the Gulf through Destin and Fort Walton Beach. The beach of Fort Walton Beach is actually on Okaloosa Island, a barrier island at the southern end of Choctawhatchee Bay. Destin is about five miles east on U.S. 98 (sometimes called the Miracle Strip Parkway). To get to this area from the north, take U.S. 331 south, then take Highway 85 south at the Alabama/Florida line, straight into Destin and Fort Walton Beach. From I-10, exit onto Highway 85 south at the Fort Walton Beach exit.

The Beaches of South Walton communities are about 35 miles west of Panama City Beach, along Highway 30A (also called Scenic 30A and Scenic Gulf Coast Drive). Highway 30A splits off from U.S. 98 just before Highway 393 in the west and right after Panama City Beach in the east.

Panama City Beach is on a barrier island. If you're visiting, note that Panama City Beach and Panama City are two separate cities and their names should not be used interchangeably. The Hathaway Bridge crosses St. Andrews Bay and connects the two of them. U.S. 98 splits at Panama City Beach and becomes U.S. 98 in the north (also called Panama City Beach Parkway) and U.S. 98A along the beach (also called Front Beach Road).

BY AIR

The nearest airports to Destin and Fort Walton Beach are the **Northwest Florida Regional Airport** (1701 Hwy. 85 N., on Eglin Air Force Base, 850/651-7160), a small airport serviced by Delta Airlines, American Eagle, Northwest Airlines, US Air Express, and Continental, and the **Northwest Florida Beaches International Airport** (6300 West Bay Pkwy., Panama City, 850/763-6751), the first international airport built in the United States in a decade and served by Delta and Southwest Airlines. A 50-minute drive to the west, the **Pensacola International Airport** (2430 Airport Blvd., Pensacola, 850/436-5000) is the biggest airport in northwest Florida. It's not huge, serving a moderate number of flights from Air Trans, American Eagle, Continental, Delta, Northwest, and US Airways. Delta has the largest number of direct flights.

Car-rental agencies are inside the main terminal entrance at Pensacola International Airport across from baggage claim. **Alamo** (800/327-9633), **Avis** (800/831-2847), **Budget** (800/527-0700), **Dollar** (800/800-4000 domestic, 800/800-6000 international), **Hertz** (800/654-3131), and **National** (800/227-7368) are all on the premises. Enterprise and Thrifty are off-site.

BY BUS AND TRAIN

As of this writing, the **Amtrak** (800/872-7245) Sunset Limited service was not operating in this area due to damage Hurricane Katrina caused to the tracks in New Orleans. You need wheels to get around locally. **Greyhound** (800/231-2222) has a bus station in Panama City (917 Harrison Ave., 850/785-6111), but public transportation won't get you to most places along the Emerald Coast, unless you're just hanging out on the beach in Panama City Beach.

THE EMERALD COAST

ALABAMA GULF SHORES

You might be asking why beaches of the Alabama coast are included in a guide about the Florida Gulf Coast. All you have to do is drive west from Florida toward Alabama and you'll see why. If the Flora-Bama, that famous ramshackle bar and restaurant, wasn't located right on the border crossing, you wouldn't even know you had just passed from one state to the other. The beaches in **Gulf Shores** and **Orange Beach** are just as beautiful and sugar-white as the more well-known stretch of coast to the east in Pensacola and Destin. Locals who live in the border region decide to spend the day out at Pensacola Beach or the Gulf Shores Public Beach based on what the weather is doing and what type of beach they feel like visiting.

From Orange Beach to Gulf Shores you have more than 32 miles of beautiful shoreline. If you aren't paying attention, you won't know that you have moved from one city to the other. Orange Beach and Gulf Shores are favored by younger travelers looking for a party and also by families who prefer plenty of entertainment, shopping, and dining options. Several new fancy-pants developments dot the island. The western end of Gulf Shores, where you find the larger golf and beach resorts, is a little more upscale. However, there are still plenty of reasonably priced accommodations, and when compared to the Florida Gulf Coast to the east, these two cities are often a real bargain.

For something more laid-back, take the ferry from the western tip of Gulf Shores and cross Mobile Bay to **Dauphin Island,** a fairly quiet and charmingly Southern destination without the traffic jams and beach parties

© JOSHUA LAWRENCE KINSER

HIGHLIGHTS

LOOK FOR ◖ TO FIND RECOMMENDED SIGHTS, ACTIVITIES, DINING, AND LODGING.

◖ **Florida Point Beach:** The ample parking is free and you have more than 6,000 feet of sugar-white sand on the Gulf of Mexico to pick a spot to park your beach chair. What more could you ask for (page 63)?

◖ **Gulf Shores Public Beach:** This is the most popular beach in Gulf Shores. There's a cluster of entertainment and restaurants surrounding it, with The Hangout at the center of the action. It's a beach party atmosphere and a perfect place for people watching (page 65).

◖ **Gulf State Park Pier:** This is the largest pier on the Gulf Coast. It extends more than 1,500 feet into the emerald waters of the Gulf and is the best place in the area to reel in Spanish mackerel, bluegill, and more. If you don't want to fish, you can pay a small fee and enjoy the views and watch the anglers pull in their "big one" (page 71).

◖ **Hugh S. Branyon Backcountry Trail:** You can hike or bike through rare maritime forest habitat, past unique freshwater spring-fed lakes, and explore beautiful dune and coastal environments on this exceptionally maintained and mostly paved trail system (page 67).

◖ **Bon Secour National Wildlife Refuge:** This preserve of more than 7,000 acres provides habitat for migrating birds, sea turtles, and other animals that rely on this fragile coastal environment. There are miles of pristine beach and an exceptional network of hiking trails to discover (page 67).

◖ **Fort Morgan State Historic Site:** Located on the western tip of Gulf Shores, this fort that played a vital role in the Civil War can be explored by foot. The park hosts reenactments throughout the year, so check the calendar if you want to see a live battle at the fort, with cannon firings and all (page 72).

◖ **Dauphin Island Audubon Bird Sanctuary:** Walk the boardwalks and trails at this sanctuary that provides important habitat for birds on their spring and fall migrations. Over 370 species have been spotted on Dauphin Island, and this is the best place to go for a chance to see them (page 84).

◖ **Fort Gaines:** This fort on the eastern tip of Dauphin Island played an integral role in the Battle of Mobile Bay during the Civil War. Walk back in time as you explore the intricate arched tunnels and high bastions (page 86).

that are typical of Gulf Shores in the summer. The beaches aren't quite as nice and the offshore oil rigs are an eyesore. However, it's the perfect place to rent a house for a weekend, a week, or more and spend every second with the family enjoying quiet sunsets and walks on the beach.

This stretch of coast was settled in the late 1800s by fisherfolk and farmers who were drawn to the undeveloped land and the easy access to a variety of freshwater and saltwater fishing environments. Early farmers grew a variety of crops, predominantly Satsuma oranges, which is the explanation for the name Orange Beach. However, you won't see many orange trees around here today. In 1920 a salesperson selling orange tree seedlings infected with blight wiped out most of the orange groves. The building of the Intracoastal Waterway in the 1930s brought more commerce and development into the area and put the region on the map as a popular vacation spot for residents of the Southeast. Today the region is visited by more than one million travelers a year, most of them coming from the Birmingham, Alabama, and New Orleans area.

PLANNING YOUR TIME

Travelers typically come to the area for weekend-long vacations, with the number of tourists swelling during the summer holidays. However, there is plenty to keep you busy for a week or more. It's not difficult to find a condo or house that is rented by the day, week, or month. During the slow winter season, you can find exceptional deals on rentals by the month or for the entire season, which typically runs November-March, with prices going up slightly around the winter holidays. The busy season is during the hot summer months mid-May-late September. My favorite time to visit this area is in the late fall, October-November, or the late spring, mid-March-mid-April.

During the fall you have cooler weather, less crowded beaches, the fall bird migrations, and better prices on accommodations, activities, and food. However, June-November is considered hurricane season, and so the weather can be unpredictable. During this time of the year, I don't recommend booking week or month-long rentals too far in advance, but if you can escape for a weekend and know the coast is clear of hurricanes, then this is a great time to be here.

The spring is even better. The hurricane season is far away and the summer crowds haven't poured in yet. The weather is cool, and the hotels and rentals are less expensive. The result is beautiful, comfortable warm weather and the beaches and forests all to yourself. This is the best time to camp and enjoy outdoor activities like paddling and hiking. The bugs, particularly mosquitoes, have just started hatching but are far from intolerable. A main concern when pursuing outdoor activities during this time are the afternoon thundershowers. They often produce violent lightning storms that are beautiful and thrilling, yet extremely dangerous. The thunderstorms happen nearly every day, usually right around 2pm.

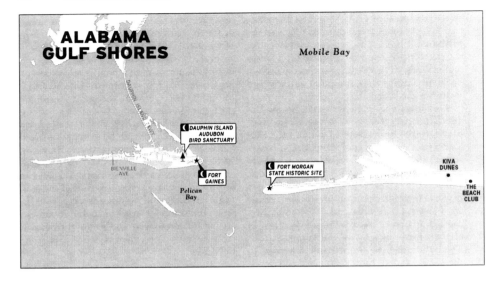

Orange Beach and Gulf Shores

This stretch of Alabama's Gulf Coast is known as "Pleasure Island." It's not a natural island. In 1933 the Intracoastal Waterway was built, which cut the beaches off from the mainland of Alabama and left this 32-mile stretch of beach surrounded on four sides by water. If you visit you'll understand why the "pleasure" part is relevant. This has been the go-to destination for Alabamians wanting a beach vacation for generations.

The biggest draw of this area—apart from the miles of sugar-white beaches—is the abundant freshwater and saltwater fishing. Dotting the coast is an impressive collection of saltwater and freshwater spring-fed lakes. Most of these lakes are found within the 6,150 acres of Gulf State Park, which also features rare maritime forest, coastal beaches, and vital dune habitat. Most of the park is concentrated around the 900-acre Lake Shelby, and as you drive along the coast, you will discover large stretches of beach and dune habitat that are preserved as a part of the Gulf State Park complex. These

preserved sections of beach are possibly the only thing that has kept this coastline from becoming entirely developed.

In more recent years the laid-back charm of the culture coupled with the exceptional value along this stretch of coast has been drawing record-breaking crowds to the area from all over the country. A boom in development occurred following Hurricane Ivan in 2004, which absolutely devastated this stretch of coast, the eye of the storm passing over Perdido Key just a few miles to the east. Several new high-rise condo developments were built on Gulf-front lots where smaller hotels and homes used to sit prior to the storm. This expanded capacity for tourists and the development of new entertainment districts like the Wharf in Orange Beach, which boasts the tallest Ferris wheel in the Southeast, have built what used to be an afterthought into a top-of-the-list destination.

If you drive down from the north on Highway 59, you will literally dead-end at the emerald waters of the Gulf of Mexico. Right

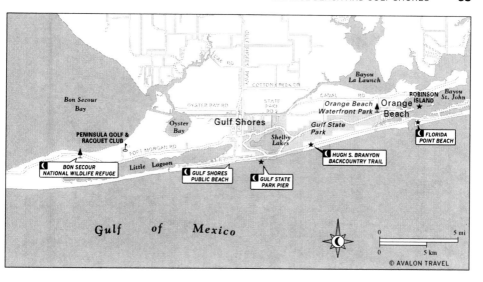

in front of you is The Hangout, a sprawling bar and restaurant favored by the party crowd, and more importantly the Gulf Shores Public Beach, which is the most popular and crowded beach on this stretch of coast. Turn right and you'll head toward the western tip of Gulf Shores, where you'll find several upscale resorts and much quieter beaches along the coast. All the way at the western tip of the island is Fort Morgan, a large fort used most famously in the Civil War during the Battle of Mobile Bay. You can take a self-guided tour of the fort, and it shouldn't be missed if you love history. Also at the western tip is the ferry terminal that can transport you or your car over Mobile Bay to Dauphin Island. If you turn right at the end of Highway 59, you will drive toward Orange Beach and the Florida border and pass by several excellent beaches with ample parking.

BEACHES
Orange Beach
You can easily access the beach from many locations around Orange Beach. Often the difficult part is finding parking, especially in the busy summer months. The best place to start is at the large parking areas and popular beaches

dotted along this stretch of coast that are a part of the Gulf State Park beach system.

FLORIDA POINT BEACH
Heading from east to west, the first beach you'll reach is the beach at **Florida Point**, located just 0.3 mile east of the Perdido Pass Bridge. The beach is wide here, and there is more than 6,000 feet of Gulf beach to walk and find that perfect spot in the sugar-white sand. Parking is free and so are the restrooms and showers. The beach sits on the eastern side of Perdido Pass, so it isn't the best spot for swimming due to the strong currents, heavy boat traffic, and higher presence of sharks in the pass. The beach does offer an excellent spot to watch incoming charter fishing boats at the end of the day.

ALABAMA POINT BEACH
Cross the Perdido Pass Bridge to reach the beach at **Alabama Point.** You can park along the west side of the bridge and walk down to the beach. This is the site of the ultra-hip Gulf Restaurant, built from two shipping containers. The owners of The Gulf have big plans for this stretch of beach. Alabama Point is slated

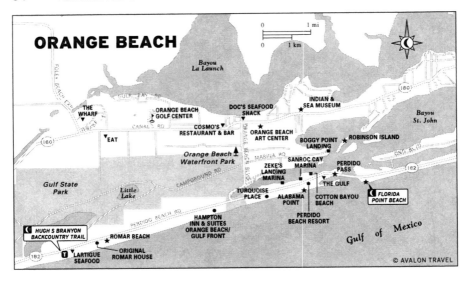

for expansion. Plans call for a much larger boardwalk complex to be built that will include beach and bait shops. Alabama Point has historically been the most popular spot for surfing, but word on the beach is that the recent dredging by the U.S. Army Corps of Engineers has ruined the break. It's still one of the best spots on the Alabama coast to catch a wave, which isn't saying much—this area isn't particularly known for its sweet surfing.

COTTON BAYOU BEACH

Just two miles west of Alabama Point at the intersection of Highway 182 and Highway 161 is the Gulf State **Cotton Bayou Beach.** This small beach access point and parking lot is easy to miss. It's located between two condo developments and is a testament to Orange Beach's dedication to providing as much public access to the beach as possible. A small restroom is located in the parking lot. Like many of the beaches in this area, Cotton Bayou is an excellent spot for swimming.

ROMAR BEACH

Head two miles west of Cotton Bayou Beach to reach **Romar Beach.** There's only a small

amount of free parking here and no restrooms or facilities. However, there are plans for development at this beach, so keep an eye out for new pavilions and restrooms in the years to come. Despite the lack of facilities at this beach, it's usually pretty busy in the summer and is an excellent spot for swimming.

ORANGE BEACH WATERFRONT PARK

The **Orange Beach Waterfront Park** (26425 Canal Rd., 251/981-6039, www.obparksandrec. com, open daily, free admission) on Wolf Bay is a favorite for families. The beautifully maintained and landscaped park has plenty of outdoor activities to keep the kids entertained. The 400-foot fishing pier extends into Wolf Bay and features covered pavilions with seating at the beginning, middle, and end of the pier. The playground is lit at night, and it's so huge and impressive that it's officially called the "kid's park." There are enough slides, swings, and things to climb on in this castle-themed playground to make any kid feel like a princess or king for a day. You'll find grills and picnic tables underneath the covered pavilions and a paved walking path for riding bikes, jogging, or taking a leisurely stroll beside the picturesque Wolf Bay.

There are 32 miles of beaches from Orange Beach to Gulf Shores.

© JOSHUA LAWRENCE KINSER

ROBINSON AND BIRD ISLANDS

Ever wanted to hang out on your own island? You can do that in Orange Beach, but you'll need your own boat to get there. In 2003 the city of Orange Beach purchased **Robinson and Bird Islands,** two small islands within a stone's throw of one another located just north of Perdido Pass. The islands and their quartz-white beaches have been a popular destination of boaters for years. On a nice summer day, boats are often packed around the island as close as possible. The official line from the city is that the islands were preserved to protect them from development and to provide a refuge for wildlife, but the most common wildlife you'll see on these islands are locals partying on the beaches.

Gulf Shores

You won't have a hard time finding a great beach in Gulf Shores. Like Orange Beach and Pensacola to the east, this area has plenty of public access points and parking lots that make

getting your beach gear to the edge of the Gulf a breeze. Many of the beaches in Gulf Shores are also a part of the Gulf State Park complex, which boasts more than three miles of preserved beaches along this stretch of coast.

◖ GULF SHORES PUBLIC BEACH

The most popular beach in the area is the **Gulf Shores Public Beach** (100 Gulf Shores Pkwy., 251/968-1420, www.gulfshoresal. gov, open daily, $5 parking). To find huge crowds of beachgoers, just drive to the end of Highway 59. The public beach is right where The Hangout is located, which is impossible to miss. There are volleyball courts, plenty of bars and restaurants in the area, three open-air pavilions, as well as restrooms with showers. It's where the young beachgoers hang out, and it usually draws more of the party crowd. This is a beautiful beach that is well maintained and regularly cleaned by the city of Gulf Shores. Lifeguards are here all day during the summer, making this an excellent choice for families and those with little swimming experience looking to challenge the Gulf of Mexico riptides with a bit of summer swimming, surfing, or boogie boarding. The beach is wide, which makes it easy to find a spot to set up the beach chair for the day, even when huge crowds are packing the beach on summer weekends and holidays. However, you might not have as much luck with parking during these times. Get here early if you need a parking spot, otherwise ride a bike or walk from your hotel or condo.

Surrounding the main public beach is a cluster of smaller public access points (251/968-1420, www.gulfshoresal.gov): **2nd St. Beach Access** (240 W. Beach Blvd., open daily, $5 parking), **5th St.** (599 W. Beach Blvd., open daily, free parking), and the **6th St. Beach Access** (699 W. Beach Blvd., open daily, $5 parking). If you're staying nearby, you can access the beach via the crosswalks at 4th Street and 13th Street as well.

GULF STATE PARK PIER

If you want to get some fishing in with your beach-lounging, a good place to start is the

ALABAMA GULF SHORES

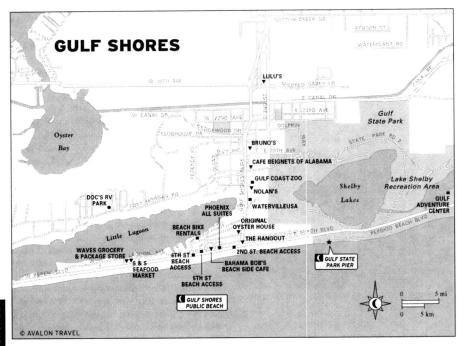

Gulf State Park Pier (20800 E. Beach Blvd., 251/967-3474, www.alapark.com, open daily, free parking), located in Gulf State Park between Gulf Shores and Orange Beach. Hurricane Ivan destroyed the original pier in 2004, and five years later Gulf Shores opened the largest pier on the Gulf at 1,540 feet long. If you don't feel like fishing, you can walk the length of the pier or just enjoy the view for $3 per adult (free for kids). Newly added to the pier is indoor seating and air-conditioning to the concession area that sells snacks and drinks, an indoor shop with tackle and bait as well as souvenirs, restrooms at the midway point of the pier, and wheelchair-accessible rail fishing. Parking is free, and the parking lot can hold over 200 cars. At the base of the pier, you will find a restroom with showers and shaded picnic tables and benches. While the pier is extremely impressive, the beach is the main attraction. The beach is wide around the pier, with plenty of room to spread out and enjoy

the sand with the family. The break around the edge of the pier pilings is popular with surfers and boogie boarders, while the rest of the beach is excellent for swimming.

GULF STATE PARK PAVILION AREA
Another top spot to hit the beach is the **Gulf State Park Pavilion Area** (22250 E. Beach Blvd., 251/968-7296, www.alapark.com, open daily, $5 parking), located six miles east of Highway 59. This beach is usually a bit less crowded than the beach around the pier, and it's a popular spot for surf fishing. Hurricane Ivan destroyed the original pavilion here, but the new pavilion is a major improvement, featuring restrooms with air-conditioning and private showers, a small snack bar, and a fireplace for cold days on the coast. It's $5 to park for the entire day, $12 for large vans. This is a great beach for families who don't mind the crowds on the weekends.

LAKE SHELBY RECREATION AREA

If you want a beach that is a little less crowded and don't mind leaving the Gulf, the beach at the **Lake Shelby Recreation Area** (20115 E. State Hwy. 135, 251/948-7275, www.alapark. com, 7am-sundown daily, free parking) is a good choice. Located just one mile east from the junction of Highway 59 and Highway 182, the beach can be accessed from the Gulf State Park campground. The 900-acre freshwater lake is open to fishing, boating, kayaking, and swimming. At the beach you'll find restrooms, showers, picnic tables, and pavilions.

BON SECOUR NATIONAL WILDLIFE REFUGE

Solitude can be found on the beaches of the **Bon Secour National Wildlife Refuge** (12295 Hwy. 180, 251/540-7720, www.fws.gov/bon-secour, 7am-sundown daily, park office 7am-3:30pm Mon.-Fri., free parking). The refuge has miles of beaches within the park, and they can be accessed by driving down the main park road, Mobile Street, until it ends at a parking lot on the Gulf, or you can hike the Pine Beach Trail to a more secluded and quiet beach to the east of the main beach area. Either way, once you are on the Gulf there are miles of beaches to walk and explore. You shouldn't have a hard time finding your very own slice of paradise where you can sit and hear nothing but the waves crashing against the shore.

HIKING, BIKING, AND WILDLIFE-WATCHING

Orange Beach

◖ HUGH S. BRANYON BACKCOUNTRY TRAIL

There are few coastal trail systems in the Southeast that are much better than the **Hugh S. Branyon Backcountry Trail** (trailheads located on Hwy. 182 and Hwy. 161 in Orange Beach, 251/981-1180, www.backcountrytrail. com, daylight hours daily, free admission). This trail system has six different trails that total more than 11 miles. The Backcountry Trail is very popular with hikers, bikers, and joggers. It's a great way to spend the afternoon exploring

the unique maritime forest habitat of Orange Beach. Construction was completed on the trail complex in 2003, and it has been a huge hit with visitors and locals. Download the free app on their website to get an up-to-date map with virtual kiosks along the way that give details on the natural surroundings, local lore, Native American heritage, and historical significance of the areas that you'll hike or bike through. Each of the six trails within the trail system traverses through a unique habitat. The most popular trail is the Catman Road segment. This paved trail is perfect for biking or hiking. It takes you past a screened-in pavilion where you can have a picnic lunch before exploring the butterfly garden and ending at the northern edge of Little Lake. This is a great way to get some exercise and spend a little time in the shade if the beach has burned you out for a bit.

You can rent bikes for the trail at **Beach Bike Rentals** (22989 Perdido Beach Blvd., 251/968-1770, www.beachbikerentals.net, 9am-sunset daily). They offer single three-speeds and cruisers as well as tandem cruisers and have daily and weekly rates. Locks and helmets are included with rentals—a huge plus that will keep the kids safe on the paved sections of the Backcountry Trail.

Gulf Shores

◖ BON SECOUR NATIONAL WILDLIFE REFUGE

Some of the best hiking in the area is found at the **Bon Secour National Wildlife Refuge** (12295 Hwy. 180, 251/540-7720, www.fws. gov/bonsecour, 7am-sundown daily, park office 7am-3:30pm Mon.-Fri., free parking). This 7,000-acre preserve contains more than six miles of hiking trails through various coastal habitats that include beaches and sand dunes, fresh- and saltwater marshes, freshwater swamps, and upland forests. More than 370 different bird species have been seen inside the preserve boundaries including ospreys, great horned and eastern screech owls, yellow-billed cuckoos, and common loons. The refuge is one of the largest undeveloped stretches of land on the Alabama coast. It receives more than

COURTESY OF JACKIE ISAACS/USFWS

Alabama beach mouse at Bon Secour National Wildlife Refuge

100,000 visitors every year, but most of them get no farther into the refuge than the popular Gulf-side beach. Once you get out on the trails, you often have the backcountry to yourself. Bon Secour means "safe harbor" in French, and today the meaning couldn't be more appropriate. While hiking in the refuge, you're likely to encounter the many migrating and resident birds that live in and visit the preserve. You might even be lucky enough to spot a red fox or coyote on your hike. If you're walking the beaches on the Gulf side May-October, you may encounter loggerhead and Kemp's Ridley sea turtles that use the beaches of the preserve as an important nesting ground.

All of the trails are located in the preserve's Perdue Unit, with one of the most popular hikes being the two-mile-long **Pine Beach Trail**. This trail provides the perfect overview of the preserve. The trailhead is near the entrance of the park on the left side of Mobile Street. The hiking is moderately strenuous, especially along the exceptionally sandy areas, where your ankles and calves will really get a

workout. Hikers traverse through the maritime scrub forest and pass between two lakes on the way to the dunes ecosystem that leads to the beach and the Gulf. The most unique and impressive section of the trail is where you hike along a thin strip of land and have the freshwater Gator Lake and the saltwater Little Lagoon on either side of you. The trail usually takes about two hours, but there's so much of interest along the way that it is easy to spend three or four hours on this hike. It's also easy to make a day of the trip and spend hours sitting or walking on the beautiful beach at the Pine Beach Trail's southern end. Another popular trail is the one-mile-long **Jeff Friend Trail** at the eastern end of the preserve's Perdue Unit. This trail is wheelchair accessible and loops around the northern edge of Little Lagoon. The hiking is easy, and along the way you'll explore sections of the maritime forest. The **Centennial Trail** connects the Jeff Friend Trail to the Pine Beach Trail and leads through the forest just north of Little Lagoon. Hike the **Gator Lake**

Trail if you want to explore the shoreline of freshwater Gator Lake. During the winter this trail is favored by bird-watchers, who often spot yellow-rumped warblers and blue-gray gnatcatchers. And if you're lucky you might spot an endangered Alabama beach mouse. Look for them scurrying across the sand dunes. They play a vital role in the health of the sand dune ecosystem by distributing seeds for sea oats, grasses, and other vegetation.

ALABAMA COASTAL BIRDING TRAIL

If you're into bird-watching, you can find the flocks by following the **Alabama Coastal Birding Trail** (trailheads located on Hwy. 182 just across Perdido Pass, 877/226-9089, www.alabamacoastalbirdingtrail.com, daylight hours daily, free admission). Detailed maps and information on all the best places to search for seabirds, sparrows, and other species can be found on their website. The site details exactly what birds you can expect to find during the different seasons in each location along the trail, which is especially helpful if you're checking off birds from your life list. The trail extends across much of Alabama, so if you want to just keep on birding, there's nothing stopping you. Much of the trail in this area is located in the Bon Secour National Wildlife Refuge and around Fort Morgan on the western end of the island. This region draws huge numbers of migrating birds during the spring and fall migrations. The birding around here is exceptional, but you can see even more birds by heading over to Dauphin Island to the west, which is considered to be one of the premier birding spots in the country.

GOLF
Orange Beach

Before you hit the course, you can practice your swing and get golf gear at the **Orange Beach Golf Center** (4700 Easy St., 251/981-4653, www.obparksandrec.com/golfcenter, 7am-9pm daily, $3/bucket). This driving range and pro shop has 30 grass tees and 10 covered mat tees. The range is lighted for driving in the cooler nighttime hours during the summer.

Gulf Shores

The Peninsula Golf and Racquet Club (20 Peninsula Blvd., 251/968-8009, www.peninsulagolfclub.com, open at 7am daily, greens fee $72 before noon, $59 after noon), a 27-hole championship course designed by Earl Stone, is tucked away beside Mobile Bay and the Bon Secour National Wildlife Refuge. Golfers of all skill levels can enjoy this extremely playable course with over 7,000 yards from the championship boxes. Winding through live oaks and native vegetation, the course attracts a wide variety of birds and wildlife that add a touch of nature to your golfing experience. The tennis courts, pools, activities at the clubhouse, and restaurant will keep the whole family occupied and happy during and after the game.

The **Gulf State Park Golf Course** (20115 Hwy. 135, 251/948-4653, www.alapark.com, open at 7am daily, 18-hole $35, 9-hole $25, discounted rates for seniors) is an exceptional value in a beautiful setting. PGA pro Harry Dwyer manages this course nestled right in the middle of a wildlife refuge. Alligators are often spotted on the lakes and water features of the 18-hole championship course designed by Earl Stone. Opened in 1972 the course has been a family tradition and a destination of golfers traveling to the area for over 40 years. The fairways are wide and there aren't too many water features, which makes playing the course a little easier than some of the other courses in the area. This a great place to bring the kids for a few rounds with the folks.

An exceptionally manicured course with impressively low rates is found at **Kiva Dunes Golf Course** (815 Plantation Rd., #100, 888/833-5482, www.kivadunes.com/golf.php, open at 7am daily, rates from $65). Designed by Jerry Pate, the course was voted Best New Course by *Golf Digest* magazine in 1995, the year it opened. You can stay at the Kiva Dunes Resort and almost walk from your room right onto the course. They frequently offer specials at the resort like a three-night package that includes two days of unlimited golf, breakfast, and cart rentals at a deeply discounted rate, so you can get the most out of a golf vacation on one of the best courses in the area.

Formerly called the Gulf Shores Golf Club, **The Golf Club at the Wharf** (520 Clubhouse Dr., 251/968-7366, www.golf.gulfshores.com, open at 7am daily, rates from $59) underwent a major renovation in 2006 under the supervision of father and son team Jay and Carter Morrish. The par-71 course was lengthened by 300 yards, and many more bunkers, water features, and fairway enhancements were added. The ProLink Solutions GPS system allows golfers to quickly get familiarized with the course with five sets of tees that range from 4,866 to 6,919 yards.

The two courses at **Craft Farms Golf Club** (3840 Cotton Creek Circle, 251/968-7500, www.craftfarms.com, open at 7am daily, rates from $59) were designed by Arnold Palmer. The Cotton Creek Course is a traditional 18-hole 7,000-yard-long course with rolling fairways and forward tees. Surrounded by lakes and forest, the four-star course has been rated by *Golf Digest* as one of the best places to play. Bring your A game to this course and relish in the challenge of the sixth hole, which requires a well-placed tee shot over water. The Cypress Bend Course has staggered tees and is rated 4.5 stars by *Golf Digest*. The sprawling bunkers, wide fairways, and vast landing areas are punctuated with cordgrass lakes that come into play on almost every hole. The fourth hole is the one to watch out for on this Palmer course. The dress code is relaxed on both courses. Golfers can wear shorts, and collared shirts and spikes are required. Groups of five are welcomed if they keep up with the pace of play.

CANOEING AND KAYAKING
Orange Beach

The best place for paddlers to start in Orange Beach is to take a trip down the **Orange Beach Kayak and Canoe Trail.** You can download maps of the 10 official launch points along this trail at the Orange Beach Community Website at www.orangebeach.ws. The trail starts at the launch on Gulf Bay Road on Wolf Bay. Paddlers travel east past Waterfront Park and Harrison Park before reaching Arnica Bay and paddling into Bayou St. John, ending at the Boggy Point Boat Launch. There are launching and take-out points along the way if you want to paddle the trail in shorter sections.

If you need a kayak for your own self-guided tour, **Paddled By You Kayak Rentals** (26448 Cotton Bayou Dr., 251/752-9250, paddledbyyou.com, 10am-6pm daily, single kayak $45/day and $10/hour, double kayak $60/day and $15/hour) will rent you a kayak to take down the trail or to launch from wherever you like. They also rent paddleboards and special kayaks outfitted for kayak fishing.

Gulf Shores

A favorite paddling and kayak-fishing spot is the spring-fed freshwater **Lake Shelby**, which can be accessed from the Gulf State Park campground. During large storms and hurricanes, the Gulf will often breach the lake and deposit saltwater fish species. This gives kayak-anglers an opportunity to experience the best of freshwater and saltwater fishing and reel in largemouth bass, speckled trout, redfish, and bluegills from Lake Shelby. The mile-long **Little Lagoon** offers great paddling, as does nearby **Gator Lake.** Paddlers can launch their kayaks and canoes from the new Lagoon Park.

The legendary **"Ice Box" on the Bon Secour River** is a favorite of paddlers. This spring head stays nice and cold year-round and is the perfect retreat from the summer heat. You can rent a kayak and take an easy self-guided float down the slow river at **Beachnriver Kayak Rentals** (Foley, 251/971-8359, www.beachnriverkayakrentals.com, 7am-3pm Tues.-Sun. May-Aug., single kayak $35, double kayak $75, for 7 hours), which launches floats from the river's end just 15 miles north of Gulf Shores. Kayakers must return to the launch site by 3pm. The rental center only accepts cash, so don't drive all the way out there and ruin the chance to float down the river by only bringing credit cards.

For renting kayaks and paddleboards on the beach, just call **GoGo Kayaks** (921 Gulf Shores Pkwy., 251/752-5500, www.gogokayaks.com,

9am-5pm daily, single kayak $55/day and $105/week, double kayak $70/day and $130/week, paddleboard $150/week). You can pick up your rentals at their shop or they'll deliver to your rental house for an extra charge. They offer daily and weekly rentals and can accommodate rentals for groups of 50 plus. Another great place to rent kayaks, or anything else you may need for your beach vacation, is **Gulf Shores Beach Rentals** (3873 Gulf Shores Pkwy., 888/896-9854, www.gulfshoresalbeachrentals.com, open daily, single kayak $95/day, double kayak $125/day, paddleboard $150/day, beach umbrella $40/day). They not only rent kayaks but also beach chairs, cribs, bicycles, umbrellas, and more. They will even do your grocery shopping if you ask them to, and pay them of course.

FISHING

In addition to the Gulf State Park Pier, you can enjoy surf fishing all along the beaches on the Gulf side, freshwater fishing at the inland lakes, and saltwater light-tackle or flats fishing in the surrounding bays, bayous, and saltwater lakes.

Orange Beach

Distraction Charters (Orange Beach Marina, 251/975-8111, www.distractioncharters.com, 8am-6pm daily) specializes in deep-sea and inshore charters for up to six people. Charters are three, four, and six hours and can be tailored to catch just about whatever you would like to catch. If it's running, Distraction Charters will help you get it.

A popular charter company geared for larger groups of seven or more is **Intimidator Charters** (Orange Beach Marina, 251/747-2872, www.gulfshoresdeepseafishing.com, 8am-6pm daily, $1,000 for 4 hours and $1,600 for 6 hours for 1-10 people). Call **Brown's Inshore Guide Service** (Orange Beach Marina, 251/981-6246, www.brownsinshore.com, 8am-6pm daily, $350 for 4 hours and $500 for 6 hours for 2 people, $50 each additional passenger) if you want to do some light-tackle inshore fishing. The knowledgeable and experienced Captain David Brown will take groups on

four- and six- hour fishing trips. All trips include bait, tackle, and fishing licenses.

If you have your own boat, you can launch at **Boggy Point Boat Launch** (end of Marina Road off Hwy. 161, 251/981-6039, www.obparksandrec.com, sunrise-sunset daily, free), near the Perdido Pass Bridge, or at the **Cotton Bayou Boat Launch** (Hwy. 182 just east of the Hwy. 161 intersection, 251/981-6039, www.obparksandrec.com, sunrise-sunset daily, free).

Gulf Shores
◖ GULF STATE PARK PIER

The **Gulf State Park Pier** (20800 E. Beach Blvd., 251/967-3474, www.alapark.com, open daily, free parking, fishing rod rentals $1.50/hour), located in Gulf State Park between Gulf Shores and Orange Beach, is the largest pier on the Gulf at 1,540 feet. That's more than a quarter-mile long. The pier can get crowded on weekends and holidays, but there is usually a spot available where you can wet your line and reel in a variety of fish species like ladyfish, king mackerel, Spanish mackerel, cobia, sheepshead, jack crevalle, speckled trout, flounder, redfish, bluefish, and black drum. The octagon-shaped end of the pier is more than 90 feet wide and offers lots of space for anglers to fish in the 26-foot-deep water of the Gulf. The snack bar, bait and tackle shop, and fish cleaning facilities that are scattered along the pier are nice additions to the new pier, which was rebuilt and reopened in 2009 after Hurricane Ivan destroyed the previous pier in 2004. A major improvement is the addition of restrooms at the midway point of the pier. Fishing passes are $8 for the day, $40 per week, and $320 per year.

FISHING CHARTERS

The best choice if you're looking to charter a fishing boat that caters to families is **Miss Brianna Fishing Charters** (26619 Perdido Beach Blvd., 251/747-3126, www.gulfshoresfishingcharter.com, 8am-6pm daily). They offer light-tackle and heavy rod fishing trips that last 4-36 hours. The 36-foot *Infinity* sleeps up to six for longer overnight charters,

ALABAMA GULF SHORES

and the cockpit is comfortable and air-conditioned, with a flat-screen TV and marine satellite dish. On the deck you can grill up your catch or whatever else you want on the onboard Big Green Egg grill while you troll and search the Gulf for yellowfin tuna, swordfish, amberjack, snapper, and more. This charter is the top choice for families and serious anglers alike.

If you want to see the charter boats and meet the captains before you book your fishing trip, you can head down to **Zeke's Landing Marina** (26619 Perdido Beach Blvd., 251/981-4007, www.zekeslanding.com, open daily). Stop by in the morning or around sunset for the chance to see one of the largest charter fleets on the Gulf Coast. The six-acre complex has several restaurants, apparel shops, and **Mo Fishin Bait and Tackle** (26641 Perdido Beach Blvd., Ste. 16A, 251/981-3811, www.topguntackle.com, open daily), where you can get all your live bait, gear, and any other fishing needs. You can also get tackle and pick up your groceries, beer, and just about anything else you need for a day at the beach at **Waves Grocery and Package Store** (1154 W. Beach Blvd., 251/948-4010, 7am-11pm daily).

SIGHTS
Orange Beach
ORANGE BEACH ART CENTER
You can explore and buy the work of local artists at the **Orange Beach Art Center** (26389 Canal Rd., 251/981-2787, www.orangebeachartcenter.com, 10am-4pm Mon.-Sat., free admission). Housed in an old homestead right on Mobile Bay and surrounded by beautiful low-hanging oak trees, this picturesque art center features paintings, crafts, pottery, and glasswork by the area's best local and regional artists. Hands-on workshops suitable for adults and children are offered in many art forms including glassblowing and are a great way to spend a rainy day when the beach isn't in the forecast.

INDIAN AND SEA MUSEUM
The small yet exceptionally interesting **Indian and Sea Museum** (25850 John M. Snook Dr.,

© JOSHUA LAWRENCE KINSER

The Indian and Sea Museum in Orange Beach explores the Native American and fishing heritage of the area.

251/981-8545, www.obparksandrec.com, 9am-4pm Tues. and Thurs., free admission) offers insight into the area's history with an emphasis on the role that Native Americans and anglers played in the rich past of Orange Beach and Gulf Shores. Housed in an old schoolhouse built in 1909, the museum opened in 1995 and quickly became a hit with locals and visitors. Make sure and allow some time to enjoy the wonderful collection of artifacts and memorabilia that fill the shelves and walls of this unique museum.

Gulf Shores
◖ FORT MORGAN STATE HISTORIC SITE
One of the most important battles of the civil war was fought at the **Fort Morgan State Historic Site** (51 Hwy. 180, 251/540-5257, www.fortmorgan.org, 8am-5pm daily, $7 adults, $5 students and seniors). The fort can be explored on foot and is a must-see for

anyone interested in the Civil War or history in general. Stop in at the visitors center and museum and pick up a self-guided tour brochure. Wonderful interpretive plaques along the route give detailed accounts of the construction of the fort and information about life at the fort during various wartimes with an emphasis on the Battle of Mobile Bay. Located all the way on the western end of Gulf Shores, Fort Morgan was the site where Union Admiral David Farragut spoke those famous words, "Damn the torpedoes, full speed ahead!" The fort contains more than 40 million bricks and was completed in 1834. The fort has seen its share of action and was active during four wars: the Civil War, Spanish-American War, and World Wars I and II. It can get a little spooky walking around in the more enclosed sections of the fort, and young children may not enjoy those parts of the fort.

The star-like shape of the fort is very interesting and unique. The design enabled soldiers to defend the main ship channel into Mobile Bay with a steady stream of artillery fire as attacking ships approached the entrance and then moved into the bay. You can also explore the old lighthouse keepers quarters on-site, which were built in 1872. Surrounding the fort are great opportunities for fishing, shell searching, or beach walking and relaxing. Also nearby is the ferry that takes you across the bay to Dauphin Island. The fort is a favorite spot to watch the sunset, and the boat launches at Fort Morgan are an excellent place to launch your watercraft into the bay or the Gulf.

ENTERTAINMENT AND EVENTS
Orange Beach

The central spot for entertainment in Orange Beach is unarguably **The Wharf** (4720 Main St., 251/224-5297, www.alwharf.com). Located on the Intracoastal Waterway, also known as Portage Creek, which feeds into Wolf Bay and the Gulf, you won't miss it if you drive down the Foley Beach Expressway. Just look out for the South's largest Ferris wheel, and you'll know that you've found the right place to do some shopping, catch a movie, see a concert, or eat a great meal. There are more than 10 different restaurants in the development, most of them catering to seafood lovers. From the expansive marina you can boat up and rent a slip for the night or catch a fishing charter and take a sight-seeing cruise for dolphins. The Wharf is also the location of the popular **Amphitheater at the Wharf,** which hosts world-class concerts. The 2013 lineup included Kenny Chesney, Kelly Clarkson, and The Fray, just to give you an idea of the caliber of musicians that perform at this picturesque outdoor amphitheater. If you're into music, make sure and check the listings at the Amphitheater while you're in town. You never know who will be coming through. You can catch a movie at the state-of-the-art **Rave at the Wharf Orange Beach.** The theater has 15 screens and matinees for those rainy days in paradise. Also at the Wharf is the indoor laser tag center called **Arena the Next Level.** You and the kids can run around more than 10,000 square feet of obstacles and structures playing laser tag or something called bazooka-ball, a game where players compete at shooting glow-in-the-dark soft foam balls from adjustable-velocity guns. It's great fun and a high-energy game that will get your heart racing.

Over at the SanRoc shopping center, you can take the family on a dolphin sightseeing adventure with **Dolphins Down Under** (Sanroc Marina, 27267 Perdido Beach Blvd., 251/968-4386, www.dolphinsdownunder.net, 8am-6pm daily, $20 adults, $15 children 3-10, children under 3 free). They specialize in family trips aboard their glass-bottom boats. The knowledgeable staff knows exactly where to go to find dolphins, and often you'll have the opportunity to see them jumping out of the water.

If you just have to squeeze in a game of mini-golf and go-carts into your beach vacation, bring the kids to **Adventure Island** (24559 Perdido Beach Blvd., 251/974-1500, www.adventure-island.com), where you can see the live erupting volcano. Ok, it's a fake volcano in a kitschy mini amusement park, but it's still neat.

ALABAMA GULF SHORES

© JOSHUA LAWRENCE KINSER

The Ferris wheel at the Wharf in Orange Beach is the tallest in the Southeast.

If that's not enough, they also have laser tag, bumper boats, and paddle boats.

Gulf Shores

Families will have a hard time running out of things to do in the Gulf Shores area. For some soaking-wet fun at a classic water park, bring the kids to **WatervilleUSA** (906 Gulf Shores Pkwy., 251/948-2106, www.watervilleusa.com, hours vary, $32.95 general admission, $25.95 military, $20.95 seniors and children under 42 inches). It's not a massive water park like you might find in a bigger city, but they have your typical waterslides that send you and your children careening down slides at phenomenal speeds, a lazy river, and other rides that are often found at county fairs, like a carousel and roller coaster. The indoor arcade offers relief from the heat on a summer day, and the food prices are extremely reasonable for an amusement park. You can make an entire day out of it, especially if you break it up with a trip to the beach or a nap for the younger kids, but

a half day is just about right for most visitors. The water park is closed for much of the winter and their hours change month-to-month. Make sure and check their website for the most up-to-date information on their operating hours.

A new addition to the Gulf Shores area is the **Gulf Adventure Center** (21101 Hwy. 135, 251/948-9494, www.gulfadventurecenter.com, $59-79). A series of high-elevation platforms connect six ziplines, two of which race over the edge of Lake Shelby. If you're not into the high adrenaline of zipping, you can take things a little slower and rent a kayak or paddleboard from their on-site outfitter. For a more classic adventure, take the family to the **Gulf Coast Zoo** (1204 Gulf Shores Pkwy., 251/968-5731, www.alabamagulfcoastzoo.org, 9am-4pm daily, $10 adults, $8 seniors, $7 children). This small zoo sits on 30 acres just blocks from the beach and houses more than 290 animals. Opened in June 1989, the zoo has continually expanded and in 2013 added a pair of Bengal tiger cubs, which made this zoo the first in the country to have tigers from each of the species' four color variations. Along with the tigers you'll enjoy the lions, bears, monkeys, macaws, a petting zoo, reptile house, and aviary. In the summer, stop by and see their daily animal shows. This park that makes a great half day of family fun.

If you're in town on the second weekend in October, make sure and stop by the **National Shrimp Festival** (along Hwy. 182, 251/968-7220, www.alagulfcoastchamber.com, $59-79). Widely considered one of the best seafood fests in the country, it attracts more than 250,000 people each year for a little peel-and-eat or deep-fried-decapod fun. It doesn't matter how you prefer to eat this area's most celebrated crustacean, you can find them served any way you like at this shrimp celebration that features over 250 vendors, local artists and musicians, and a 10k/5k run in the morning.

If you want to hold your own private film fest, you can spend the day watching movies at the **Cobb Theaters Pinnacle 14** (3780 Gulf Shores Pkwy., 251/923-0100, www.cobbtheatres.com/pinnacle14). And the best way to learn about the fascinating history of the area is to spend some time at the **Gulf Shores Museum** (244 W. 19th Ave., 251/968-1473, www.gulfshoresal.gov, 10am-5pm Tues.-Fri., 10am-2pm Sat., free admission). Learn about the area's fishing history and how Gulf Shores has coped with intense and destructive hurricanes in the past at this small but interesting and informative museum.

SHOPPING
Orange Beach
Shopping is pretty limited to surf shops, beach-goods stores, and souvenir shops along most of the main drag, but you can find a nicer collection of mostly beach-themed boutiques at **The Wharf** (4720 Main St., 251/224-5297, www.alwharf.com). Another similar development built around a large marina is the **SanRoc Cay Marina Entertainment District** (27267 Perdido Beach Blvd., 251/981-5423, www.sanroccay.com). More of an extension of the Perdido Beach Resort, this shopping district features concerts by local musicians on weekends in the courtyard. The shops are all locally owned and mostly sell women's beach-themed apparel, art, and gifts. Four restaurants are on-site, and you can rent kayaks and Jet Skis, take fishing excursions, and enjoy dolphin cruises right from the marina docks.

To really dig in deep to your desire for great deals, all you have to do is drive to the **Tanger Outlet Center** (2601 S. McKenzie St., Foley, 251/943-9303, www.tangeroutlet.com/foley) in Foley, Alabama. This enormous outlet mall features factory stores like Gap, Jos. A. Banks, J. Crew, and more, and is just 20 minutes or 18 miles from Orange Beach. For groceries, you can go to **Publix** (25771 W. Perdido Beach Blvd., 251/980-1400, www.publix.com, 7am-10pm daily).

Gulf Shores
All your surf gear and apparel needs can be met at **Innerlight Surf Shop** (3800 Gulf Shores Pkwy., 251/948-4222, www.innerlightsurf.com, 10am-7pm Mon.-Sat., noon-6pm Sun.). A local favorite for more than 40 years, Innerlight has a huge inventory of surfboards, surf shorts,

wax, and anything else you may need to catch a wave and hang 10—or at least appear as if you do. For the ultimate selection of bikinis and souvenirs, stop in at **Alvin's Island** (100 W. Beach Blvd., 251/948-3121, www.alvinsisland.com, 9am-midnight daily). This beach-goods megastore has an impressive inventory of everything you could possibly need or want for the perfect day at the beach (and a lot more stuff that most people don't need). The best prices on groceries are usually found at **Bruno's Grocery** (1545 Gulf Shores Pkwy., 251/968-4911, www.brunos.com, 7am-10pm daily). There's also a Winn-Dixie and a Publix in the area if you have a preference or just need one of those perfect Publix deli sandwiches to pack for a beach picnic.

ACCOMMODATIONS
Orange Beach
If you're looking for a great value in the area, stay at the **Hampton Inn and Suites Orange Beach** (25518 Perdido Beach Blvd., 251/923-4400, www.hamptoninn3.hilton.com, $89-229). Breakfast and wireless Internet is included, and the suites have refrigerators and microwaves that will help you cut back on your dining bill. The inn has easy access to a Gulf-front beach, and the views from some of the rooms are excellent. The 160 guest rooms have nice, modern decor and those comfy signature beds that I always want to take home every time I stay in one. There's over 3,750 square feet of meeting space, enough to accommodate more than 300 people, which also makes this property a great choice for conventions, business meetings, and events.

A classic resort in the area is the **Perdido Beach Resort** (27200 Perdido Beach Blvd., 251/981-9811, www.perdidobeachresort.com, $114-249). You can choose between pool-view and Gulf-front rooms, some of which are set up more for business travelers with a desk (make sure and request a room with a desk when booking if that's your preference). The piano bar in the lobby area is a favorite with locals and visitors as a great place to bring a date for a classy cocktail over jazz. The tiki-style pool

ALABAMA GULF SHORES

bar mixes up good piña coladas and margaritas with a wonderful pool-side view of the Gulf. There is easy access to the beach and an excellent indoor heated pool that makes a winter stay extremely enjoyable. The resort has four lighted tennis courts and a spacious fitness center with one of the best views of any workout room on the panhandle. And I love that there is absolutely no resort fee to stifle your fun.

Built in 2008 the **((Turquoise Place** (26302 Perdido Beach Blvd., 800/210-7914, www.turquoiseplacerental.com, $275-700) is as architecturally stunning as it is enjoyable to experience. The impressive glass condo tower is unarguably the focal point as you drive down this stretch of beach. The development was featured on the cover of *USArchitecture* magazine as one of the top projects of 2007/2008. The resort caters to both families and couples, and the Gulf of Mexico is just feet from the building. There are two heated indoor pools, an indoor children's pool, two seasonally heated outdoor pools (one of which is zero-entry), three indoor hot tubs, and—my favorite—the 450-foot-long lazy river that winds around the property. It's hard not to just swim and float your worries away at Turquoise. Stop in at the poolside tiki bar or spend the day at their full-service spa getting a massage or a luxurious body polish. The fitness center is top-notch with an excellent view of the Gulf to enjoy while you are getting your body back into summer shape. Every aspect of the resort is sleek, clean, and modern, yet without the sterility that some modern developments have unfortunately created at their high-end properties. The prices for rooms vary depending on the size, floor plan, and location, but all rooms are definitely at the high end of the price spectrum for Orange Beach. If you are looking for luxury, pampering, and an inspiring modern environment in which to spend your beach vacation, you won't be disappointed with Turquoise.

If you're looking for something a little more casual but just as relaxing, try staying at the **Original Romar House** (23500 Perdido Beach Blvd., 251/974-1625, www.theoriginalromarhouse.com, $129-329). Owners Deborah and Greg Collard run this six-room bed-and-breakfast on the Gulf. The spacious back deck looking directly over the Gulf is the perfect spot to enjoy the full breakfast they serve or just a cup of coffee in the morning. Each room has a theme and is decorated with antiques. You can stay in the colorful Mardi Gras room or the tropical-themed Parrot House Cottage with an entire kitchen and living room. The smaller Captain's Quarters is about as small as a room you would find on a ship and is perfect for solo travelers on a budget. Free wireless Internet, complimentary wine at happy hour, afternoon refreshments, and a hot tub make a stay at the Romar House a real treat. The best feature of this B&B, however, is the warm hospitality of the owners and the wonderful breakfast they serve up every morning.

Gulf Shores

The Gulf Shores area has definitely begun to lean toward more high-end development and for the most part outshines Orange Beach accommodations in this respect. However, there is still a wide variety of accommodation choices in Gulf Shores. The budget-minded traveler looking for a suitable efficiency can find a great deal at the **Staybridge Suites Gulf Shores** (3947 Gulf Shores Pkwy., 251/975-1030, www.ichotelsgroup.com, $89-159). The suites have fully equipped kitchens and are exceptionally spacious for the price. You can save a bundle having a kitchen during a long vacation with a family, and you won't have to pay for breakfast either, because a hot breakfast is served every morning. The Internet is free, and many of the rooms have a work desk. There are not a lot of frills, but you can't beat the rates for these spacious and exceptionally clean rooms in a great location.

A more upscale experience can be had at the **Courtyard by Marriott Gulf Shores Craft Farms** (3750 Gulf Shores Pkwy., 251/968-1113, www.mariott.com, $79-149). Located on the front edge of the Craft Farms Golf Resort, this property is geared to the golfer that wants to mix business with time out on the golf course playing one of the best courses in the panhandle. The rooms feature free Internet service and desks in all 87 rooms and three suites. The styling is sleek and modern, but still warm and welcoming. If you are in town for a weekend of golf and don't want to fight the traffic to the public beach four miles away, you can just enjoy their excellent pool.

For one of the best golf getaways on the Gulf Coast, stay at **Kiva Dunes** (815 Plantation Dr., 251/540-7003, www.kivadunes.com, $199-329). Surrounding an artfully designed course on the far west end of Gulf Shores is a collection of homes and condos that you can rent for a week or months at a time. If golf isn't your thing, don't worry. The beaches at this end of the island are much quieter, and Kiva Dunes has over 3,000 feet of beach to explore. There are three outdoor pools, a fitness center, an on-site restaurant, tiki bar, golf pro shop, well-maintained tennis courts, and a spacious fitness center with modern exercise equipment. In short, they have everything you need; you can just park your car and never think about driving anywhere else during your stay. The size, price, style, and layout of the homes vary greatly. However, you can see photos, prices, and the exact location of every rental property in the resort at their very detailed website so you can find the perfect place to stay, as close to the Gulf or golf course as you want.

You can choose from a large variety of cottages and condos at the **Gulf Shores Plantation** (805 Plantation Rd., 251/540-5000, www.gulfshoresplantation.com, $129-259). This resort should not be overlooked by deal seekers. Some of the smaller cottages are very affordable. Staying at any of the condos and cottages here gives you access to the full amenities of the resort, which include one indoor pool and six, yes six, outdoor pools as well as hot tubs, saunas, horseshoe pits, a putting green to keep your golf skills sharp for the days at any of the 10 courses in the area, and thousands of feet of Gulf beaches. The resort is very family oriented and has tennis courts, shuffleboard, and basketball courts as well as a fitness center for the more active ones in the family. All the cottages and condos are fully equipped with everything you need for cooking and relaxing, and all the units have either a patio or balcony. Free Internet service is included with the rentals, and there is a variety of floor plans and sizes to accommodate almost any budget.

My personal favorite place to stay in the area is ❰ **The Beach Club** (925 Beach Club Trail, 251/224-3200, www.thebeachclub.spectrumresorts.com, $219-459), located just to the east of Kiva Dunes on the west end of Gulf Shores. This is the perfect place for families. Each of the cottages and condos has a fully equipped kitchen, and all the condos have balconies with views of the Gulf. The condos range 1-5 bedrooms. They are all privately owned, but the website for the resort makes it easy to browse through the individual units and find a style, size, and price that is perfect for you. If you have the time you can really find a great deal on a condo, especially in the off-season. The cottages are a little more luxurious and give you the privacy of renting your own home while still allowing you access to the resort's amenities. Many of the cottages are situated around a lake, and some have expanded kitchens, hot tubs, and even private pools. The clubhouse has live music most nights, and there are several outdoor pools around the resort if you need a break from the beach. Organized kids' programs and activities including craft projects, scavenger hunts, and team sports games will keep the young ones busy throughout the day. A full-service spa and hot tubs will keep you relaxed, and you can grab a cold ice cream at the on-site ice cream shop. It is a classic beach resort that is geared toward families. Every corner of the resort has something entertaining and fun happening to keep those short attention spans engaged.

Vacation Rentals

The large majority of vacation rental companies in the area deal with properties in both Orange Beach and Gulf Shores. There is a wide range of homes and condos available for rent in the area, with most of the homes suitable for large or small families and running the gamut from simple, classic, modest beach cottages to impressively large and fancy beach homes big enough for several families to share. All along the coast are high-rise condo developments. The amount of offerings can be overwhelming, but a few of the expert rental companies in the area can help you get exactly what you are looking for, whether it is a small condo right on the Gulf or a large home tucked away on a wooded lot on Mobile Bay. The two most well-established and trusted rental companies in the area are **Meyer Vacation Rentals** (1585 Gulf Shores Pkwy., Gulf Shores, 800/213-9544, www.meyerre.com) and **Brett/Robinson Vacation Rentals** (3259 Gulf Shores Pkwy., Gulf Shores, 251/968-7363, www.brett-robinson.com), serving both Gulf Shores and Orange Beach. Either of these companies can get you headed in the right direction, and both have great websites with pictures and prices of all the homes available in the area.

An upscale selection of Caribbean-style cottages and condos can be found at **Martinique on the Gulf** (987 Boulevard Martinique, Gulf Shores, 855/858-6950, www.martinique-gulf. com, $250-575). This premier development is adjacent to the Bon Secour National Wildlife Refuge and offers a mix of two- and three-bedroom condos and two- to five-bedroom cottages. The idyllic resort environment is reminiscent of Seaside and WaterColor to the east and features a phenomenal pool area with a hot tub and kid's pool, a fitness center, professional tennis courts, and a private boardwalk that leads to the Gulf beaches. The two-story French colonial-style cottages will have you feeling as if you have been whisked away to the Caribbean.

Located in the middle of town are the **Phoenix All Suites Hotels** (533 W. Beach Blvd., Gulf Shores, 251/968-4900, www.phoenixallsuites.com, $130-250). The west and east towers feature one-bedroom suites with full kitchens. You can choose between the standard one-bedroom, one-bath floor plan or a unit with 1.5 baths. Each unit has a balcony with a view of the Gulf and a fully equipped kitchen. They're no-frills condos, but the price can make these clean yet somewhat utilitarian condos look much better. The nice outdoor pool and the fact that the condos are just 1,500 feet from the public beach make the Phoenix a great value.

Camping

The best camping in the Gulf Shores and Orange Beach area is at **☾ Gulf State Park** (22050 Campground Rd., Gulf Shores, 251/948-7275, www.alapark.com/gulfstate, 7am-sunset daily, $34.41 campsite, $85-177 cabins, $212-232 cottages). This 496-site campsite is located along the north shore of Middle Lake and offers many lakefront campsites. The sites are very close together, which makes the campground better suited for RV or pop-up camping. Some sites offer more privacy and shade for tent camping, but the size of the campground and the close proximity of sites can often lead to a loud camping experience. If you're tent camping and a light sleeper, make sure and bring some earplugs because during the hot summer months RV campers often run their air conditioners at night, which can be quite loud. The campground offers direct access to miles of hiking trails, including the Rosemary Dunes Trail, which leads to the Gulf of Mexico and the Gulf State Park Pavilion Beach. If you don't want to hike the trail to get to the beach, it's just a 1.5-mile drive from the campground. And if you just don't think you can handle roughing it out on the beach for a few days, you're in luck. This campground offers more comforts than most. The swimming pool, wireless Internet, modern and clean bathhouse with hot showers, full laundry facility, and water, electric, and sewer hookups at every site will make you feel like you're staying at a nature-based eco-resort instead of a campground. The lake is open for swimming, fishing, and boating, and the campground is within walking distance of the Gulf State Park Golf Course.

If sleeping in a tent or RV just isn't your thing, the park offers even more comfort in their cabin and cottage rentals. The park has 20 cabins and cottages, which are mostly one- and two-room buildings that sleep 4-6 people. They are located along the lakeshore, near the golf course, and a few in a forested area of the campground. The cabins on the lakeshore are some of the best in the park. Each has a private dock, fish cleaning bench, and barbecue grills. Each cottage is fully equipped and linens are provided. The cabins are reserved far in advance, so make sure and book yours way ahead of time if you hope to enjoy some of the most comfortable camping you've ever experienced.

On the bay side in Gulf Shores, you can pull your RV into **Fort Morgan RV Park** (10397 2nd St., 251/540-2416, www.baybreezerv.com), where 35 sites are spread over six acres right on Mobile Bay. Large oak trees provide ample shade at most of the campsites, and nearly every site has a water view of the bay. This park is favored by anglers, who can fish from the 200-foot pier. Beaches are just 1.5 miles from the park. Water, sewer, electric, cable, and wireless Internet are included with each site, which run $35-49 depending on the water view. A little more tucked away and on the northern side of Little Lagoon is **Doc's RV Park** (17595 State Rd. 180, Gulf Shores, 251/968-4511, www.docsrvpark.com, $33 daily, $205 weekly). They have 75 RV sites and are only three miles from the beach. Each site has full electric and sewer hook-ups, wireless Internet, and cable. The campground features a swimming pool, playground, laundry, bathhouse, clubhouse, and 14 cabins you can rent if you don't own an RV. This campground is a favorite among long-term seasonal campers. They offer daily, weekly, and monthly rates. And 25 more RV sites can be found in Gulf Shores at **Bay Breeze RV** (1901 Bay Breeze Pkwy., 251/540-2362, www.baybreezerv.com, $36-48 campsites, $89-109 RV sites, $110-135 cottages). Beach access on Mobile Bay is just a short walk from the campground. They also offer RV rentals and one cabin to rent. The fishing and boat dock make this campground the choice of boaters. The campground has a bathhouse and laundry facility, making it more comfortable to stay here for a longer period of time.

FOOD
Orange Beach
The Gulf (27500 Perdido Beach Blvd., www.thegulf.com, 11am-midnight daily, $8-20) is tops on the Orange Beach restaurant scene. It's built from two stacked shipping containers, but the artfully executed building design turned what could've been an eyesore into a masterpiece of modern architectural design. Even if you're not hungry, stop by for a drink and enjoy the excellent view of the Gulf of Mexico. The menu is a welcomed departure from the "fry everything" edict that dominates the Orange Beach culinary culture. The selections manage to put a fresh twist on tired seafood dishes. Cheeseburgers, grouper sandwiches, and cold-cut hoagies keep the less-adventurous satisfied while dishes like lobster spaghetti and crawfish tacos bring fresh flavors to the oceanfront dining options.

Hot sauce and cold oyster aficionados will love **Doc's Seafood Shack** (26029 Canal Rd., 251/981-6999, www.docsseafoodshack.com, 11am-9pm daily, $7-16), where everything you need to custom mix your own cocktail sauce creation is sitting right on the table, and where the best oysters on the half shell are found. If you're looking for a place to eat where you would feel overdressed in anything nicer than swim shorts and a Guy Harvey tee, then you've found the right spot. Doc's is as casual as a cracker barrel and a favorite of folks who prefer fried food. It's also the perfect place to relax and watch the game with the family while you work your way through a pound of fried shrimp, a few dozen raw oysters, and gallons of really good sweet iced tea.

A new twist on the all-you-can-eat buffet can be found at **Eat** (4401 Money Bayou Dr., 251/974-2328, www.staycationscatering.com/eat, 11am-3pm Mon.-Fri., $10-20). They serve up a rotating menu with enough variety to keep you coming back every day of your vacation. The menu changes daily and usually features comfort foods along with a salad and dessert bar. Expect items like broiled chicken, mash potatoes, green beans, black-eyed peas, and cherry cobbler one day, then spicy jambalaya,

© JOSHUA LAWRENCE KINSER

Fresh roses decorate every table at The Gulf, an innovative Orange Beach restaurant constructed from shipping containers.

boiled crawfish, okra, and chocolate pudding the next. The decor is sleek, clean, and comfortable, and the food is of infinitely better quality and much healthier than you usually find at buffets. If you want quality food and have a large appetite for Southern and Creole cooking, go to Eat.

((Cosmo's Restaurant and Bar (25753 Canal Rd., 251/948-9663, www.cosmosrestaurantandbar.com, 11am-9:30pm Sun.-Thurs., 11am-10pm Fri.-Sat., $15-30) also features classic New-Orleans-inspired eats. At lunch try the redfish encrusted with pecans, or go simple and enjoy a muffaletta, po'boy, or crab cake sandwich. At dinner savor the French influence with the chicken roulade, a chicken breast wrapped in bacon and then stuffed with asparagus and gruyère cheese, topped with a sage-and-leek cream sauce. Their signature dish is banana-leaf-wrapped fish, and their sushi menu is extensive. Make dinner reservations on weekends during the summer. If the weather's cool and

clear, sit on their outdoor patio. The lines can be long, but the experience is worth the wait.

For fresh and steamed carryout seafood, go to **Lartigue's Seafood Market** (23043 Perdido Beach Blvd., 251/948-2644, www.lartiguesseafood.com, 7am-9pm daily). The usual suspects such as raw oysters, fresh Gulf shrimp, snapper, and the likes can be found on ice, ready for you to take home and cook up. The family-owned market has been open in Orange Beach since 1979, and they have some of the best prices in the area.

Gulf Shores

Restaurants are plentiful in Gulf Shores, and most are found right along Highway 182, which is called Beach Boulevard, and Highway 59, called Gulf Shores Parkway. There are some real local gems, but choose wisely as there are plenty of places that prey on the unsuspecting tourist with low-quality frozen seafood and subpar service just to make a quick buck. The amount of options for food can be overwhelming, but if you only go to one place in Gulf Shores, head to **((Lulu's** (200 E. 25th Ave., 251/967-5858, www.lulubuffett.com, 11am-9pm Sun.-Thurs., 11am-10pm Fri.-Sat., $10-25). It's owned by Jimmy Buffet's sister and is a venerable shrine to the Margaritaville lifestyle. It's colorful and tropical and everything you would imagine from a place run by the sister of the king of trop-rock. The main restaurant and bar is on Portage Creek and is surrounded by a sprawling outdoor seating area complete with volleyball courts, a playground, and several smaller bars housed in Key West-style cottages. Drive in or sail your boat right up to the dock. The coconut shrimp coupled with a cheeseburger in paradise and a slice of key lime pie are the perfect pairing with your third piña colada.

Another Gulf Shores institution is **The Hangout** (101 E. Beach Blvd., 251/948-3030, www.thehangoutal.com, 11am-9pm Mon.-Thurs. and Sun., 11am-10pm Fri.-Sat., $10-25). Not a must-stop like Lulu's, The Hangout is pretty much Gulf Shores' answer to the Flora-Bama. More known as a bar than a restaurant,

© JOSHUA LAWRENCE KINSER

Lulu's serves up the finest margaritas and other frozen concoctions in Gulf Shores.

this is the place to go for a loud night out of rowdy dancing and tequila shots or to watch the day game and have a few beers with your friends over wings, burgers, and fried shrimp or other standard beach food selection from their enormous and rather pricey menu.

For an elegant dining experience, locals go to **Nolan's** (1140 Gulf Shores Pkwy., 251/948-2111, www.nolansrestaurant.com, open at 6pm Tues.-Sat., $18-28). The atmosphere is upscale, making this a great choice for a romantic dinner or just an excuse to dress up and wear something other than flip-flops and swim trunks for a night. They specialize in steaks, seafood, and Greek-inspired cuisine with standout menu selections such as a Mediterranean-style grouper baked in olive oil and lemon and served with broiled tomatoes, onions, kalamata olives, and feta cheese. For something more adventurous, try the whole flounder stuffed with crab meat and chestnut stuffing. After dinner head to the lounge and indulge in their extensive wine and martini list.

If you want to eat oysters while you're in Gulf Shores, then go to **The Original Oyster House** (701 Gulf Shores Pkwy., 251/948-2455, www.theoysterhouse.com, 11am-10pm Sun.-Thurs., 11am-11pm Fri.-Sat., $9-20). They've got oysters prepared every single way you can imagine as well as the standard seafood options like fried flounder, grouper, crab claws, gumbo, and one of those enormous platters of fried seafood that is ubiquitously known at seafood restaurants across the Gulf Coast as the fisherman's platter. It's a perfect place for a large family dinner, and the peanut butter pie is the perfect way to end a meal at this popular Gulf Shores restaurant.

Calling all parrotheads! If you just didn't get enough of the Margaritaville lifestyle at Lulu's, then continue your search for the perfect frozen concoction at **Bahama Bobs Beach Side Café** (601 W. Beach Blvd., 251/948-2100, www.bahamabobs.com, 11am-8pm daily, $10-20). A ship wreck in the Bahamas inspired Bob to move to Gulf Shores and open his own restaurant. Well-loved for their fried shrimp and po'boys, this small tropical-style café is within walking distance from the beach. That's a good thing because parking is limited. The outdoor seating is worth the wait and a better choice than the somewhat cramped indoor seating. A great pick from the menu is the shrimp and crab combo with boiled potatoes and corn. It's enough for two if you have a small- to medium-sized appetite.

For a sweet Southern-style treat, stop in at **Café Beignets of Alabama** (625 Gulf Shores Pkwy., 251/948-2311, 7am-2pm daily, $5-12), where like the name implies they serve those delectable, French-style, puffy, crispy donuts covered in a substantial layer of powdered sugar. The menu is simply beignets and coffee, which is sure to satisfy a café du monde craving without having to drive all the way to the French Quarter in New Orleans. My advice is to forgo your regular cup of joe and try the café au lait and chickory coffee that has that special Southern flavor that you don't want to miss. If you're looking for a little down-home Southern country cookin' you can't go wrong

with breakfast, lunch, or dinner at **Kitty's Kafe** (3800 Gulf Shores Pkwy., 251/943-5233, 6am-7pm Mon.-Sat., 7am-2pm Sun., $7-15), where owner Kitty Simpson will appease your craving for fried chicken and the likes. They serve breakfast all day, so don't be shy coming into Kitty's at 1pm for pancakes and bacon after a late night at The Hangout and Flora-Bama.

Are you tired of paying those high prices for a small fillet of broiled snapper, but don't quite have the angler's knack? Then take the easy road and pick up your own fresh seafood to cook yourself or order take-out seafood at **S & S Seafood Market** (1154 W. Beach Blvd., 251/968-3474, 11am-8pm daily, $5-15). The prices here are better than most of the seafood restaurants in the area, and the spicy fried shrimp, fried grouper, and gumbo are some of the best in all of Gulf Shores. You can call ahead and place your order if you want to get back on the beach in a flash, and make sure to ask for a few hush puppies on the side.

Dauphin Island

If you want to escape the crowds and hordes of tourists that you'll surely find around the Gulf Shores and Orange Beach area but still want to be on the beach, then just load your car onto the ferry at the western tip of Gulf Shores and sail on over to Dauphin Island. You can also get to the island by taking the long drive north to Mobile and then back down south to the island, but the ferry is way more fun. The island has been favored by Mobile and surrounding areas as a family vacation destination for decades, and it still remains a family-oriented getaway today. Also a favored destination by anglers in the area, Dauphin Island offers great access into Mobile Bay to the north, Bon Secour Bay to the east, and the Gulf of Mexico to the south. The fishing on the island is so good that it is home to the Alabama Deep Sea Fishing Rodeo, the largest fishing tournament in the world. The island is usually quiet, but it's transformed every

July into a bustling frenzy of anglers, fishing boats, and more than 75,000 spectators. This is definitely when the island is most lively, so if you don't want to deal with crowds, avoid setting foot on the island during the rodeo.

If I had to describe the island in just two words, I would say "laid back." The pace of life is slow on Dauphin Island, and there is a clear, obvious lack of pretension and ostentation, which can be charming to some and off-putting to others. It's an angler's and outdoorsperson's paradise and the kind of destination to visit if you're looking to do nothing but have boat drinks and work on your tan. There's hardly any shopping to speak of unless you're in the market for fresh oysters, shrimp, and blue crab, and the accommodations options are extremely limited, with most visitors renting homes or condos on the island. Dauphin Island is genuinely Southern and a place where the influences

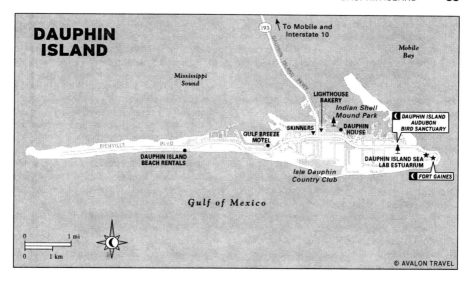

DAUPHIN ISLAND

193 ↑ To Mobile and
Interstate 10

*Mobile
Bay*

*Mississippi
Sound*

LIGHTHOUSE
BAKERY

*Indian Shell
Mound Park*

SKINNERS   DAUPHIN
HOUSE

GULF BREEZE
MOTEL

BIENVILLE   BLVD.

DAUPHIN ISLAND
BEACH RENTALS

*Isle Dauphin
Country Club*

DAUPHIN ISLAND
AUDUBON
BIRD SANCTUARY

DAUPHIN ISLAND SEA
LAB ESTUARIUM

FORT GAINES

Gulf of Mexico

0   1 mi
0   1 km

© AVALON TRAVEL

of the French and Spanish express themselves in the cuisine, culture, and architecture in a spectacular way.

While the fishing is particularly impressive on the island, the bird-watching is some of the best in the world. Dauphin Island is the first piece of land that birds usually reach during their biannual migrations. The island is considered to be one of the top 10 most significant spots on the planet for birds and was named by *Wild Bird Magazine* as one of the top four locations to watch spring migrations in the United States. On the eastern tip of the island you'll find the Audubon Bird Sanctuary, a 164-acre parcel of land that is preserved and managed to support these massive migrations that occur every spring and fall on the island. If you love birds, then grab your binoculars and come to the island in the spring to see some of the 347 species of birds that have been reported on this 14-mile-long island.

The Spanish were the first to claim the island, but the French were the first to settle here. The island was originally named Massacre Island by the French explorers Pierre Le Moyne and Sieur D'Iberville. When they first anchored off the island in 1699, they discovered a massive pile of human skeletons and believed a massacre had taken place. However, what they discovered was a Native American burial mound that had been split open by a hurricane. Maybe it was a bit of a warning because the island has had trouble with hurricanes and storms since it was first permanently occupied, but then again, that can be said for the entire Florida coast. In 1707 the name was officially changed to Isle Dauphine. Dauphin Island was briefly the capital of the French territory in the new world, but after a devastating hurricane in 1717, the French moved their capital to Pascagoula and then to New Orleans.

During the late 1700s Dauphin Island saw many changes in ownership. It was occupied by the French, British, and Spanish, and then in 1803 the United States purchased Dauphin Island as part of the Louisiana Purchase. In 1821 construction began on a new fort on the eastern tip of the island. The fort was completed in 1861, and you can still visit it today. Just drive east down Bienville Boulevard to the end of the road and you'll reach the fort. Take a self-guided tour or drive your vehicle around the fort's outer wall that runs parallel to the coastline of the island. No matter what you do when you visit Dauphin Island, you won't be able to help but slow down, and I definitely encourage you to do so. This is how the locals live, and to really experience the island you need to remember to do two things—first, take a boat out on the water, and then just relax. This is what the locals do, and they understand how to experience the best that this island has to offer.

SPORTS AND RECREATION

Beaches

More impressive than the beaches on Dauphin Island is the island's laid-back atmosphere and culture. Now don't get me wrong, the beaches are worth going to and definitely enjoyable in their own way, but the better beaches are to the east in Gulf Shores and Orange Beach. On Dauphin Island the biggest drawback is the number of offshore oil rigs close to shore, which can be clearly seen from the comfort of your beach chair. This might not bother many people, but when I look out across the Gulf, I prefer to see the clean, blue line of the horizon and not the blinking lights of an oil rig platform.

There are three main access points for the beaches on Dauphin Island. The largest and most popular beach is the **Dauphin Island Public Beach Access** (1509 Bienville Blvd., 251/861-3607, www.dauphinisland.org, $5/car or motorcycle, $2 for pedestrians or bicyclists, $20 for motor homes or buses), which is also the site of the Dauphin Island Fishing Pier. This is a beautiful beach with more than two miles of undeveloped beaches, four large picnic pavilions, restrooms, outdoor showers, and a very nice playground for children. When you first get to the beach, you'll notice two things. First, it is a long trek from your car to the edge of the Gulf where most people prefer to set up their beach chairs and umbrellas. Second, there is something extremely odd about the fishing pier. The pier never reaches the water. In fact, it doesn't even come close to reaching the Gulf. At one time this was a deepwater fishing pier. Over the course of 2007 and 2008, Pelican Island was slowly moved toward Dauphin Island by a series of harsh hurricanes

and winter storms until Pelican Island connected with Dauphin Island. Now the beach is much larger, but the pier is sadly unfishable. Make sure and wear sandals for the long trek out to the water's edge. The beach is good for swimming, but be forewarned that there are no lifeguards, so keep your swimming close to shore, look for rip currents, and avoid the Gulf when it's rough if you're not accustomed to swimming in open waters.

On the east end of the island, you can use the **Fort Gaines Public Beach Access.** It's not much of a beach, but the thin strip of sand around the fort area is a convenient place to get close to the water if you're visiting the fort. This beach is excellent for swimming, but again there is unfortunately no lifeguard on duty.

And with the pier now out of use at the main public beach, the island authority has decided to open the **West End Public Beach** (far west end of Dauphin Island, 251/861-5525, www.townofdauphinisland.org, 10am-6pm daily, $2 parking plus $3/person over 12). Opened in March 2013, this family-oriented beach has a waterslide, beach chair and umbrella rentals, food vendors, sno-cones, and cocktails. The waterslide and sno-cones are reminiscent of Pensacola Beach back in the 1970s and 1980s. The West End beach is nice and wide and is known as a great place to find the best shells on the island. A lifeguard is on duty through the summer season, making this the best beach for swimming on the island.

Birding, Hiking, and Biking

◖ DAUPHIN ISLAND AUDUBON BIRD SANCTUARY

The **Dauphin Island Audubon Bird Sanctuary** (211 Bienville Blvd., 251/861-3607, www.dauphinisland.org/audubon-bird-sanctuary, dawn-dusk daily, free admission) was created to accommodate the large number of migrating birds and butterflies that pass over Dauphin Island during their spring and fall migrations. Bring your binoculars and explore this 164-acre park on the eastern side of the island that features a wide variety of habitats. Explore freshwater lakes, swamp, beach, coastal dune, pine forest, and hardwood forest on six trails that cut through the park. The park can be accessed from the Dauphin Island Campground as well as from the main parking lot on Bienville Boulevard. Spring is the best time to come and bird-watch on the island, and it is said that birds literally fall out of the sky when a cold front with rain is pushed over the island during the height of spring migrations. If you're into birding, the Audubon Bird Sanctuary should not be missed.

INDIAN SHELL MOUND PARK

For a more historical experience, hike the trail at the **Indian Shell Mound Park** (Iberville Rd., dauphinislandhistory.org, dawn-dusk daily, free admission). The very short trail leads around an ancient shell mound left behind by early Indians that possibly used the island as a place to escape the cold winter weather. And if you really want to burn off some of those extra calories from eating too much of the Southern seafood staples found all over the island, then lace up your boots or rent a bike and hike or ride the **Island-Long Bike Path.** The seven-mile paved path runs parallel to Bienville Boulevard and traverses most of the island. With such an excellent and accessible bike path, there's no reason why you can't see everything on the island and get a great workout at the same time. Besides, the more you hike or bike on the bike path, the more fried shrimp and daiquiris you're allowed to have.

Canoeing and Kayaking

If you want to further explore the rich aquatic environment around the island, you can rent a kayak from the **Dauphin Island Marina Kayak Shack** (650 LeMoyne Dr., 251/861-2201, dauphinislandmarina.com, 8am-5pm Wed.-Sun., single kayak $25 for 2 hours and $50/day, double or tandem kayak $40 for 2 hours and $80/day). If you want to do some kayak-fishing you can buy your bait and tackle at the Dauphin Island Marina store. Guided eco-tours that explore the open water of the Gulf as well as the bays are also available at the Kayak Shack.

If you want a kayak or bike brought to

you, call Lynn at **Dauphin Island Kayak and Bicycle Rentals** (251/422-5285, 8am-5:30pm daily). She has been operating her bike and kayak delivery service for more than 10 years on the island. Single kayaks are $25 for two hours and $60 for a full day. She also rents tandems and has the best prices on kayaks if you're looking at renting two or more boats for more than two days. Bicycles are $15 per day. Lynn also offers tours of the island by boat or bike. Her tours can include lunches at one of the local restaurants or pre-packed picnics if you prefer.

Now that you've rented a boat you can launch your watercraft at one of the many boat launches or beaches around the island. On the eastern side of the island you can launch at the Dauphin Island Campground or the boat launch at Fort Gaines. These are great launches to paddle out to Sand Island just south of Dauphin Island in the Gulf. The boat launch at the Dauphin Island Marina is centrally located and an excellent launch point into Mobile Bay. And it's easy to get into the Gulf from the main public beach that is centrally located on the south side of the island.

Fishing

Right before you get on the island, you can pick up all the fishing supplies you need and learn a little bit of the locals' secrets by stopping in at **Jemison's Bait & Tackle** (16871 Dauphin Island Pkwy., 251/873-4695, 5am-8pm daily). The ramshackle store might not look like much, but it offers a wealth of information if you ask the right people. Just past the store, you can put your newly purchased bait and tackle to the test at the **Cedar Point Fishing Pier** (18250 Dauphin Island Pkwy., 251/873-4476, www.fishingpier.net, 24 hours daily, $5 admission). You can buy tackle and bait at the fishing pier's shop as well. A great place to fish late into the night, the pier is the oldest privately owned fishing pier on the Gulf Coast, and it's been getting a lot more business since the Dauphin Island Fishing Pier has become unfishable. You can still walk out on the Dauphin Island Fishing Pier, but if you try and fish from this "pier," the only thing you'll be catching is sand crabs and the occasional tourist.

If you want a pro guide to take you out into Mobile Bay or any of the surrounding fishing hot spots, just call **Capt. Mike's Deep Sea Fishing** (650 LeMoyne Dr., 251/861-5302, www.captainmikeonline.com) to set up a fishing charter. He is based out of the Dauphin Island Marina and has three boats that range 40-65 feet. They can accommodate you whether you want to do some trolling and bottom fishing for red snapper, king mackerel, and grouper or just want to go after the big boys and try to reel in a blue marlin or record-setting tuna.

SIGHTS
Indian Shell Mound Park
Visit the **Indian Shell Mound Park** (Iberville Rd., 251/861-2882, www.dauphinislandhistory.org, dawn-dusk daily, free admission) and walk the short trail through the 11-acre park that circles around a massive shell mound left behind

by early Native Americans who must have really loved oysters. They roasted boatloads of these yummy bivalves and threw the shells into a pile that over time grew to the highest point on the island. Almost as impressive as the mound are the enormous oak trees found in the park. Some of the larger oak trees are more than 800 years old and were mature trees when the Spaniards first visited Dauphin Island.

◖ Fort Gaines
Arguably the most historically significant site on Dauphin Island is **Fort Gaines** (51 Bienville Blvd., 251/861-6992, www.dauphinisland.org/fort.htm, 9am-5pm daily, $6 adults, $4 children 5-12), located on the eastern tip of the island. Construction of the fort began in 1821 and was finally completed in 1861. The fort was used most notably in the Battle of Mobile Bay, one of the most significant battles of the Civil War. During World War II, the fort became a station for an anti-submarine branch of the U.S. Coast Guard as well as the base for the Alabama National Guard.

Explore the fort and cannons of Fort Gaines at the eastern end of Dauphin Island.

After paying the entrance fee at the visitors center, you are free to explore the fort on your own. Constructed with brick and sand mortar, the fort's most notable features are the tall arched tunnels and steep outer walls. In and around the fort are original cannons, a functioning blacksmith shop, kitchens, and an exhibit that includes the original anchor from the USS *Hartford,* where Admiral David Farragut spoke the famous words, "Damn the torpedoes, full speed ahead!" Even though the fort has received substantial damage from the ongoing tropical storms and intense hurricanes, it is still considered one of the best-preserved forts from the Civil War era, with excellent examples of early artillery.

Dauphin Island Sea Lab Estuarium

To learn more about the Mobile Bay aquatic environment, visit the **Dauphin Island Sea Lab Estuarium** (101 Bienville Blvd., 919/861-2141 http://estuarium.disl.org, 9am-6pm Mon.-Sat., 1pm-6pm Sun., $10 adults, $8 seniors, $6 children 5-18). The primary focus of the estuarium is to facilitate Alabama's universities and grade schools with courses, workshops, and graduate programs in marine-science environmental education. However, the public can get a glimpse into what life is like below the waters of Mobile Bay, the Tensaw River Delta, and the northern Gulf of Mexico by visiting the estuarium and exploring the indoor visual exhibits as well as taking a walk on the boardwalk above the surrounding marsh. While exploring the estuarium, you will see alligators, turtles, snakes, gars, oysters, horseshoe crabs, blue crabs, stone crabs, shrimp, octopus, eels, starfish, seahorses, and jellyfish. The highlight of the facility is a touch tank that lets children touch sea life on display. The kid-centric aquarium and environmental education programs will get children of all ages interested in understanding what is happening in Mobile Bay, the fourth-largest estuary system in the United States.

EVENTS

The biggest festival on the island is the **Alabama Deep Sea Fishing Rodeo** (251/471-0025, www.

adsfr.com). Held in mid-July, this fishing tournament has been active for more than 79 years and is the largest multi-species saltwater fishing tournament in the world, attracting more than 3,000 anglers and upward of 75,000 spectators every year. Even if you're not competing in the tournament, it's a ton of fun to watch the boats come in and unload their impressive catches onto the docks. The three-day event awards over $400,000 in prizes in 30 categories including a master junior angler award.

The **Art Fest in the Park** (Cadillac Square, 251/861-5524, www.dauphinislandcoc.com) is a juried art show featuring local and regional artists. In recent years the art festival has been combined with the Back to Nature Festival, which integrates a schedule of outdoor activities that promote environmental awareness. Spend the day strolling under the oaks enjoying displays of artwork in Cadillac Square and then join a boat tour, animal exhibition, or nature walk at this multi-themed festival.

Ever wonder what life on Dauphin Island was like before Fort Gaines was built? You can find out at the **Colonies of the Gulf Coast** (Fort Gaines, 251/861-6992, www.dauphin-island.org/fort). This living-history day at the fort includes live reenactments by soldiers, pirates, and period craftsman, as well as some very exciting live cannon firing.

Most people consider New Orleans to be synonymous with Mardi Gras, but the festival actually began in Mobile. You can experience Mardi Gras Dauphin Island-style at the **Island Mystics Parade** (Bienville Blvd., 251/861-5525 ext. 222, www.townofdauphinisland. org). Always the second parade of the season, which usually occurs sometime in mid- to late January, the parade is much more laid-back than the parades in Mobile or New Orleans. You won't find any barricades, but you will see families cooking out and partying along the parade route for the entire day, and usually into the late hours of the night. Crowds arrive very early along the route to stake out and set up their camps for the day. So if you have dreams of catching piles of beads and stacks of MoonPies (those delectable, chocolate-covered,

.am-cracker-and-marshmallow-stuffed eats that are tossed out at parades), you better get to the parade early in the morning before the first float rolls past.

SHOPPING

There's not much of a shopping scene in Dauphin Island, but there is plenty of island-themed clothing, jewelry, and other beach souvenirs at **Marti's Island Shoppe** (1606 Bienville Blvd., 251/861-8772, 10am-4:30pm daily). A nice collection of sea life-inspired art, gifts, and clothing can be found at the very popular **Dauphin Island Sea Lab Estuarium Gift Shop** (101 Bienville Blvd., 251/861-2141 ext. 7545, giftshop.disl.org, 9am-6pm Mon.-Sat., 1pm-6pm Sun.). You don't have to pay the admission fee to get into the gift shop, and if you like Gulf-themed housewares it is worth a stop.

You can find all the groceries and other beach supplies you need at the **Ship & Shore** (401 LeMoyne Dr., 251/861-2262, 5am-9pm daily), located just across the bridge on the right as you come onto the island. This grocery store doubles as the town's hardware store, too, so they should have just about everything you could ever need while you're in town. If you're in desperate need of retail therapy, you'll want to head over to Gulf Shores or Mobile.

ACCOMMODATIONS

Accommodations are extremely limited on Dauphin Island, and most visitors rent beach houses or condos during their stay.

Under $100

The best affordable choice on the island is the **Gulf Breeze Motel** (1512 Cadillac Ave., 251/861-7344, www.gulfinfo.com/gulfbreeze-motel, $59-119). Family owned and operated since 1982, this no-frills motel with free Wi-Fi access is located on the bay side and within walking distance to the public beach access. You can enjoy views of the bay from the balconies of most of the motel's 32 rooms. Two rooms are suites with full kitchens, and when you combine the motel's low rates with the ability to cook your own meals, you end up with an

The Gulf Breeze Motel is one of the few lodgings on Dauphin Island.

extremely affordable beach vacation. The prices vary greatly from month to month, so make sure and check with them about their current rates. The only rooms more than $100 are the two suites, and this is only during the busy summer months. The dock behind the motel has boat slips if you want to sail or boat up to your room. You can't see the Gulf of Mexico from your room, but it is such a short walk away that you can avoid fighting traffic and searching for a parking space and instead enjoy every minute possible out on the beach during your stay at this clean, comfortable, and highly recommended motel.

$100-150

For an enjoyable bed-and-breakfast experience on the island, stay at the **Dauphin House Bed and Breakfast** (730 Cadillac Ave., 251/391-4073, http://dauphinhouse.com, $89-130). Owners Carol and George Clark are extremely knowledgeable about the area and are known to take visitors on short tours of the island. The 10 rooms at the property vary greatly, some having larger bathrooms, more beds, or better views of the bay than others. Make sure and call and let the owners know what you are looking for so they can get you in the right room. The rooms I would recommend are rooms 8 and 10, as they have nice balconies that overlook the bay. Two rooms at the bed-and-breakfast have more than one bed and can accommodate up to four guests. The pier behind the house is a great place to fish for flounder and redfish or to use as a place just to hang out on the bay. Co-owner George Clark cooks up a wonderful breakfast every morning that includes eggs, grits, fruit, hashbrowns, and other breakfast favorites.

Vacation Rentals

The best way to set up a beach rental is to contact **(Dauphin Island Beach Rentals** (103 Treasure Ct., 251/455-1159, www.dauphinislandbeachrentals.com). They offer a wide variety of homes and condos to choose from, with most options being family-oriented beach houses that tend to be more modest in size and style than what you might find farther east.

The homes and condos that are available, the most part reflect the island's laid-back and casual attitude and lifestyle. Most homes and condos on the island rent for $75-200 per night or $500-1,500 per week. Monthly and long-term rentals are available.

Camping

The only campground on the island is the **Pelican Nest RV Resort and Campground** (1510 Bienville Blvd., 251/861-2338, www.dauphinislandcampground.com, $35-80). The campground has 150 sites with access to power and water and 75 sites with RV hookups. In the bathhouse you'll find hot showers and restrooms. A boardwalk takes you from the campground to the beach, and a small store in the campground will keep your cooler stocked with all the camping and most of the beach supplies you need. It's free to use the boat launch, and when you're not on the water, you can explore the nearby Fort Gaines historical site. The campground is only a half mile from the where the ferry departs. This is great if you want to hitch a ride over to Gulf Shores for the day, but not the best situation if you are a light sleeper or a tent camper. The ferry arrives early in the morning, and when the ferry horn blows, there is little chance you'll be able to keep slumbering peacefully. For this reason, the campground is more accommodating for RV campers, but if you're set on tent camping, then just bring a good pair of earplugs.

FOOD

It's a small island, and the selection of restaurants is unfortunately limited. Most of them are located right across the Dauphin Island Bridge on LeMoyne Drive and along Bienville Boulevard, with a cluster of choice eateries around the intersection of these two roads.

For a delightful breakfast before you hit the beach, visit the **(Lighthouse Bakery** (919 Chaumont Ave., 251/861-2253, 7am-2pm Wed.-Sun., $4-10) This historic home has been turned into a wonderful bakery that serves large, flaky croissants and a wonderful selection of fresh-made sandwiches for breakfast or

The Lighthouse Bakery is a Dauphin Island favorite for breakfast and lunch.

lunch. Eat outdoors at one of the tables that line the front porch or at the picnic tables on the front lawn if the weather is nice. If the bakery is busy, you can get effectively distracted by browsing the interesting and quirky collection of knickknacks and souvenirs they have for sale that line nearly every square inch of the restaurant walls.

If you've got a craving for barbecue, your best bet is a stop at the **Dauphin Island BBQ** (906 Bienville Blvd., 251/861-7427, 11am-8pm daily, $7-15). This spot is ultra-casual. The dining area isn't much more than a covered deck with ceiling fans. The only air-conditioning is found in the bathrooms, but all you need is a nice breeze from the Gulf and the place is comfortable on most days. The menu includes the regular fare for barbecue joints with the standard pulled pork and ribs, but then departs from the norm and includes barbecue shrimp and Creole favorites like gumbo. Remember, you're only a few hours from New Orleans. The farther west you go the spicier and more Cajun-influenced the food becomes.

A great place on the island for lunch, dinner, or a drink is **Islander's Restaurant** (1504 Bienville Blvd., 251/861-2225, 11am-2:30pm and 5pm-9:30pm Thurs.-Sun., $12-20). Formerly the Oarhouse, the new management has really turned things around and greatly improved the menu. There are fresh seafood dishes as well as some of the best shrimp po'boys on the island, with excellent, perfectly chewy rolls. The portions are large and the shrimp and grits and piña coladas are a perfect combo after spending the day on the beach.

For fresh seafood that you can cook at the beach house or condo, stop in at **Skinners Seafood** (703 LeMoyne Dr., 251/861-4221, www.skinnerseafood.com, 8am-5pm daily, $7-15). They own their personal fishing boat, and as a result nearly everything in the store is brought in fresh daily from the Gulf and bay. Just don't go into the store hungry or you might leave with more raw oysters, shrimp, and red snapper than you can handle. They also sell a nice variety of hot sauces, spices, boils, and batters to accompany your effortless seafood catch.

Information and Services

Orange Beach, Gulf Shores, and Dauphin Island are located within the **central time zone.** The telephone area code is **251.**

TOURIST INFORMATION

The **Gulf Coast News** (251/947-7712, www. gulfcoastnewstoday.com) is the best way to find out about local events and entertainment. The same company also produces the *Baldwin Times,* the *Courier,* the *Robertsdale Independent,* the *Gulf Shores and Orange Beach Islander,* and the *Foley Onlooker.* You can find kiosks at many of the grocery stores, entertainment developments, and shopping centers around the area. For visitor information on Gulf Shores and Orange Beach, stop in at the **Alabama Gulf Coast Convention & Visitors Bureau** (23685 Perdido Beach Blvd., Orange Beach, 251/974-1510) to pick up brochures and maps as well as plenty of great coupons. They also maintain a website (www.gulfshores.com) with a tremendous amount of visitor information.

Dauphin Island events and information can be found easily online at **www. dauphinislandtimes.com.** For more Dauphin Island information, call or visit the **Dauphin Island Chamber of Commerce** (1101 Bienville Blvd., 251/861-5524, www.dauphinislandtourism.com); they share a space with the community library and have free Wi-Fi, computers to use, and all the information and brochures you need to plan your Dauphin Island days.

POLICE AND EMERGENCIES

Of course, if you find yourself in a real emergency, pick up a phone and dial 911. For a non-emergency police need, call or visit the **Orange Beach Police Department** (4480 Orange Beach Blvd., 251/981-9777, www.obpd.org). The **Gulf Shores Police Department** can be

reached at 251/968-2431, and the **Dauphin Island Police Department** can be reached at 251/861-5523. In the event of a medical emergency, stop into the **Orange Beach Medical Center** (4223 Orange Beach Blvd., 251/974-3820) or **Gulf Shores Medical Center** (200 Office Park Dr., 251/968-7379). To fill a prescription there is a CVS pharmacy in Orange Beach (25761 Perdido Beach Blvd., 251/974-1590). The **Gulf Shores Pharmacy** (251 Clubhouse Dr., 251/968-3784) has an antique soda fountain and Wurlitzer jukebox to play while you wait.

RADIO AND TELEVISION

You can tune your radio station to **91.3 FM** for public radio, **94.9 FM** for country, **96.1 FM** for classic rock, **97.5 FM** for top 40 hits, or **99.9 FM** for a wide variety of music. Turn to **1350 AM** for sports talk, and either **870 AM** or **1400 AM** for news talk.

And on the television, **WPMI Channel 15** out of Mobile is the NBC affiliate, **WBPG Channel 55** out of Gulf Shores is the CW affiliate, **WKRG Channel 5** out of Mobile is the CBS affiliate, **WEAR Channel 3** out of Pensacola is the ABC affiliate, and **WEIQ Channel 42** out of Mobile is the PBS affiliate.

LAUNDRY SERVICES

Most of the hotels, condos, and resorts on Orange Beach or Gulf Shores offer their own laundry services to guests. There's also the **AAA Laundromat** (3645 Gulf Shores Pkwy., Gulf Shores, 251/948-9274) if you happen to be staying at a property without laundry machines. There's no Laundromat in Dauphin Island. However, most of the hotels and nearly all the homes and condos you can rent have access to laundry machines for a small fee.

ᵍ There and Around

ᴗAR

The main driving access to the area from New Orleans in the west and Jacksonville and Tallahassee in the east is I-10. If you're coming from the north, you can take I-65 from Birmingham or I-85 from Atlanta. All these points lead to Mobile, Alabama. To get to the Gulf Shores area from Mobile, it's 49 miles, a one-hour drive. Just follow Highway 59 South to the Gulf Shores Public Beach and turn right to go toward the west end of Gulf Shores or left to go toward Orange Beach.

The quickest way to Dauphin Island from I-10 is to take Highway 193 South to the island. If you're coming from Pensacola, simply follow U.S. 98 to Highway 292, also known as Barrancas Avenue, Gulf Beach Highway, and Sorrento Road at different points along the route. Highway 292 goes through Perdido and right to the Florida/Alabama border, where it becomes Highway 182 once you cross into Alabama and reach Orange Beach.

BY AIR

By air, the closest large airport is **Pensacola International Airport** (850/436-5000, www.flypensacola.com), one hour to the east in Pensacola. Most major domestic airlines serve the airport. The airport has enjoyed enormous growth recently; the current terminal was expanded in 2011 at a cost of $35 million. There is a smaller regional airport in Mobile, the **Mobile Regional Airport** (800/357-5373, www.mobairport.com), which offers nonstop jet service on American Airlines, Delta, United, and US Airways to Atlanta, Charlotte, Houston, and Dallas. Private planes can also fly into Jack Edwards Airport in Gulf Shores, Foley Municipal, and Dauphin Island Airport.

Thrifty (877/238-0898), **Hertz** (850/432-2345), **Avis** (850/433-5614), **Budget** (850/432-5499), **Enterprise** (850/478-6730), and **Alamo** (888/826-6893) provide rental cars from Pensacola International Airport. **Advantage Airport Shuttle** (850/420-7807, www.advantageairportshuttle.com, Pensacola to Orange Beach $60-70, Pensacola to Gulf Shores $75-90) provides service from Pensacola Airport to Orange Beach and Gulf Shores.

BY TRAIN AND BUS

Amtrak (800/872-7245, www.amtrak.com) offers train service as far south as the Hattiesburg, Mississippi, station, located 100 miles west of Gulf Shores, but you'll have to drive from there. Amtrak has plans to repair the rail line that runs from New Orleans through the Panhandle. This route has been out of service since Hurricane Katrina badly damaged the tracks in 2005. Also, **Greyhound Bus Line** (239/774-5660, www.greyhound.com) provides regular service into Mobile, and the **Wave Transit System** (251/344-6600) operates a reliable network of city buses ($1.25 fare).

MOON SPOTLIGHT PENSACOLA

Avalon Travel
a member of the Perseus Books Group
1700 Fourth Street
Berkeley, CA 94710, USA
www.moon.com

Editor and Series Manager: Kathryn Ettinger
Copy Editor: Ann Seifert
Graphics and Production Coordinator:
  Domini Dragoone
Map Editor: Kat Bennett
Cartographers: Kat Bennett and Stephanie Poulain
Indexer: Greg Jewett

ISBN-13: 978-1-61238-982-0

Text and maps © 2014 by Avalon Travel.
All rights reserved.

Laura Reiley wrote the first and second editions of
Moon Florida Gulf Coast.

Front cover photo: Beautiful ocean water with
  swimmers vacationing on beach in Pensacola,
  © Cheryl Casey | Dreamstime.com
Title page photo: Pensacola beach, © Andrew
  Zarivny/123RF

Printed in Canada by Friesens

ABOUT THE AUTHOR

Joshua Lawrence Kinser

Florida native Joshua Lawrence Kinser spends the better part of each year traveling the entire length of the state's Gulf Coast. After bouncing between jobs for more than a decade, traveling around the world as a wildlife biology research technician and a professional drummer on cruise ships, he returned to Florida to write full-time.

Joshua honed his writing skills working as a staff writer for *The Pensacola News Journal* and publishing articles for magazines such as *SAIL* and *Times of the Islands*. As a wildlife biology tech, he has worked in Florida, Hawai'i Volcanoes National Park, Glacier National Park in Montana, and in the forests surrounding Yosemite National Park in California. Passionate about the outdoors, he is always searching for the best freshwater springs, hiking trails, campsites, and fishing spots.

Joshua currently splits his time between Black Mountain, North Carolina, and Gulf Breeze, Florida.

CPSIA information can be obtained at www.ICGtesting.com
Printed in the USA
LVOW08s1242270814

400975LV00005B/28/P

9 781612 389820